Famous Frontiersmen

By

JOHN W. MOYER

FIELD MUSEUM OF NATURAL HISTORY

Illustrated by

JAMES L. VLASATY

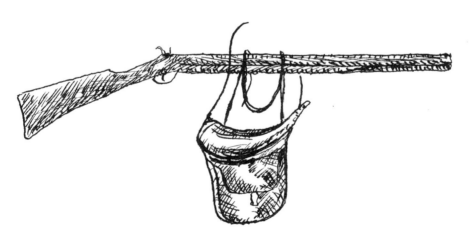

RAND McNALLY & COMPANY

Chicago • New York • San Francisco

Colt Navy/38 cal.
1851

Colt Army/44 cal.
1860

Colt Frontier/45 cal.
1873

*To those hundreds,
and possibly thousands,
of men and women*

who lived and died heroically with unrecorded deeds
of courage, personal tragedies and untold suffering,
and whose names therefore did not go down in history
either as a famous person or a famous frontiersman
in the opening of the West,
this book is humbly dedicated.

Colt Wells Fargo/31 cal.
1846

Wild Bill Hickok's Gun

Colt Walker/44 cal.
1847

Colt Texas Paterson/40 cal.
1836

CONTENTS

CHAPTER   PAGE

I   Daniel Boone   9

II   Lewis and Clark   19

III   David Crockett   32

IV   Samuel Houston   40

V   James Bowie   53

VI   James Bridger   62

VII   Christopher Carson   73

VIII   James Butler Hickok   85

IX   George Armstrong Custer   94

X   William Frederick Cody   105

Daniel Boone/Long Kaintuck

Blunderbuss/Lewis
& Clark
1741

U.S. Rifle/Lewis & Clark
1802–14

PORTRAITS

PLATE		PAGE
I	Daniel Boone	8
II	Lewis and Clark	18
III	David Crockett	34
IV	Samuel Houston	42
V	James Bowie	52
VI	James Bridger	64
VII	Christopher Carson	72
VIII	James Butler Hickok	84
IX	George Armstrong Custer	96
X	William Frederick Cody	104

Custer's Men at Rosebud/Single-shot
1876

Winchester Repeater
1873

Riding Shotgun/Double-barrel
Wells Fargo

Daniel Boone

1735-1820

JAMES W. VAASATT

I

Daniel Boone

1735–1820

One of the best known frontiersmen responsible for the early settlement of our country was Daniel Boone. Daniel Boone was born in Exeter township, Bucks County, Pennsylvania, February 11, 1735, the fourth of seven sons. He had four sisters. His parents were Squire and Sarah Morgan Boone, and his father was a man of wealth with large tracts of land in Maryland, Virginia, and later Pennsylvania.

Daniel Boone grew to manhood in primitive frontier conditions. Exeter township was a vast wilderness. What few settlers there were lived in log cabins grouped together for safety from Indian attacks. Daniel's school was the woods. He would often roam the forests miles from home, studying the ways of the Indians and the wild life. He became an expert rifleman and woodsman, able to live off the land for days, weeks, or months—a necessity in those times. This early training saved his life many times in the years ahead.

When Daniel was 17, his family moved to North Carolina, locating on the Yadkin River near Wilkesboro. At 21 Daniel married Rebecca Bryan and settled down to the life of a farmer. But a few acres of farmland could not hold Boone's interest for long. He and others like him were anxious to explore the unknown territory beyond the Appalachian range—the area that later became the state of Kentucky. Possibly another reason for his restlessness was the continued harassment of the colonists along the coastal areas by the British.

Very little has been recorded of Boone's life during the years between 1760-68. But it is known that he spent much of this time when not at farm labors exploring and becoming acquainted with the territory towards the west. Boone knew that more territory would soon have to be opened to settlers searching for land to build homes on.

At last Boone joined a party of men who wanted to build a settlement at Canaan Creek in Kentucky. After assuring his family that all would be taken care of in his absence, he headed west in May 1769. After traveling for some weeks, they reached Canaan Creek and set up camp around a crude log cabin.

This was the territory of the Shawnee, Cherokee, and Chickasaw Indians. But, as the months passed and no Indians were seen, the men lost all fear of attack. Then late in December, while Boone and a man named Stuart were hunting, they ran into a party of Indians. Realizing they were outnumbered, the two men surrendered without a struggle and allowed themselves to be taken to the Indian camp. There they managed to convince the Indians that they were really quite pleased with their captivity. The Indians became less and less watchful, and after a few days Boone and his companion were able to escape during the night. When they reached the cabin at Canaan Creek, they found it deserted and plundered by Indians. No trace of the other men was ever found.

Boone and Stuart continued to hunt and explore. But, knowing that the Indians were hostile, they were more cautious.

In January 1770 the two men were joined by Daniel's brother Squire, who brought fresh supplies, much-needed ammunition, and welcome news of their families in Carolina. Daniel had been away from his family now for eight months. Squire Boone was accompanied by another man, whose name is not known.

One day when Boone and Stuart were hunting, they were ambushed by Indians. Stuart was killed, but Boone escaped to join his brother and the other man. A few days later this unnamed hunter, too, was killed.

As the two brothers watched their companions die and their supplies running out, they must have thought of giving up. But Daniel was sure that he was exploring the boundaries of a new state. He would not be beaten by the wilderness or the Indians. When Squire went back to Carolina for supplies, Daniel continued his explorations alone. Squire returned with the supplies in July 1770, and the two brothers continued hunting and exploring the territory until March 1771, when they both returned to Carolina. Daniel had been gone for more than two years.

The Atlantic States, as they were then called, were becoming more and more settled. After several months with family and friends, Boone decided the time had come to move his family to the frontier and build a new settlement.

In September 1773 after selling the farm on the Yadkin, Daniel and Squire set out with their wives and children on their journey west. All their possessions, clothing, furniture, cattle, swine, and horses went with them. Later they met and joined a larger party of about 40 men with women and children.

Early in October, the party was nearing a mountain pass known as Cumberland Gap. Suddenly the Indians attacked the young men herding the cattle some miles to the rear. They killed six of the men and drove off the cattle. Among the slain was Daniel Boone's eldest son.

Shaken by this savage attack, most of the settlers turned back. Daniel and Squire, after returning part way, settled in southwestern Virginia, near the Clinch River. The following summer Daniel and another man led a party of surveyors to the so-called Falls of Ohio.

Daniel's fame was now established. After several other tasks of exploring and peace-making with Indian tribes, he was commissioned captain of militia by the governor of the territory. After fighting for several months in an Indian war, Captain Boone returned to his home in Virginia.

Boone by now had a reputation as a bold leader—and one determined to settle the rich land of Kentucky. The Cherokee Indians claimed this part of the country, and Boone was asked to negotiate a treaty with the tribe so that the land could be settled in safety. Boone was successful, and a treaty was signed with the Indians on March 17, 1775. Boone was now selected to open a road to the Kentucky River and to build a settlement there. In April, Boone's party reached the spot where Otter Creek empties into the Kentucky River. They camped at the site of present day Boonesborough and began to build a fort.

Indian tribes who had not signed the treaty continually attacked the men. But in June 1775 the fort was ready. Boone returned to Virginia for his family and in September he and a party of 26 men, four women, and five boys returned to Boonesborough. Boone's wife, Rebecca, and his daughter, Jemima, were the first white women ever to stand on the banks of the beautiful Kentucky River. After a few months, Boonesborough became the headquarters for all new settlers to the territory.

War with England was soon raging in the Colonies and along the coast. Many men left their homes in the wilderness to fight. Since the British had enlisted some Indian tribes as allies, the wilderness forts were in constant danger. In April and July 1777 Boone, in command of the fort, held off large parties of Indians. Months of Indian raids stopped traffic to and from the fort. Boonesborough was soon without salt—needed for preserving meat. In January 1778 Boone and 27 men went to Blue Lick to make salt from salt water. When Boone left the men to hunt for food, however, he was captured by Indians on their way to attack Boonesborough.

Boone realized that the fate of his party — and of Boonesborough, was now in his hands. He knew that, without him and his 27 men, the fort could not hold off an Indian attack. He decided to delay that attack by giving the Indians some prisoners to worry about. He surrendered his entire party at Blue Lick with the condition they would be well treated. The Indians took everyone to their village near Old Chillicothe, Ohio, on the Little Miami River. Although Boone's decision saved Boonesborough, he was later severely censured for it.

Since Boone was known to all tribes in the area, he and his men were well treated. Later all but Boone were turned over to the British at Detroit. Boone was brought back to Old Chillicothe and adopted into the tribe—an event not to his liking. It was now June and a band of Indians took Boone with them to Blue Lick to make salt. While the Indians were at the Lick, the chiefs of the tribe decided to attack Boonesborough. When this news reached Boone, he slipped away from the Indians and headed for the fort 160 miles away. Traveling without food, he made his way to the fort in time to warn the people of the danger and to again take command of the defense. He was disappointed to find that his family was

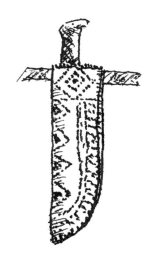

gone. Thinking that Boone had been killed at Blue Lick, they had returned to Carolina.

After Boone's escape, the Indians delayed their attack. But late in August under the command of a British officer, a large force of Indians and British surrounded the fort. The commander demanded that Boonesborough surrender and be turned over to the British. Even though the defenders of the fort were greatly outnumbered, they refused to surrender. After nine days of siege, the attackers were beaten. Boone's forces pursued the fleeing savages and won the bloody Battle of Blue Lick. This was the last important attack upon Boonesborough.

In late autumn of 1778 Daniel Boone left Boonesborough and returned to Carolina and his family. He wintered with them, and in the spring of 1779 they returned to Boonesborough. With them came settlers for other parts of Kentucky. People looked upon Boone as the founder of that state.

In 1780 Boone and his brother Squire were attacked by Indians while they were making salt at Blue Lick. Squire was killed, but Boone was again able to outwit the Indians and escape. It was also in 1780 that the militia of Kentucky was reorganized. Major Boone became a lieutenant colonel.

In August 1781 Indians from Old Chillicothe laid siege to Bryants Station, a small post on the road between Lexington and Maysville. When this news reached Boonesborough, Colonel Boone led a party of men including his brother Samuel and his son Israel, to the relief of the station. Some of Boone's officers did not follow Boone's instructions, and the party was ambushed by the Indians. In this fight Israel Boone was killed. Then for a time Kentucky enjoyed rest from Indian hostilities.

Colonel Boone used his military pay to buy several tracts of land and started farming. Then in 1790 Boone lost all his property through a technicality of law. At this time ownership of land in Kentucky was in confusion, and Boone had not made certain that his title was clear.

His farm at Boonesborough and the farms of many other settlers were lost. Now nearly 60 years old, Daniel Boone, founder of the state, found himself without a home. Boone and his wife left Boonesborough and finally settled along the Kenhawa River in Virginia near Point Pleasant.

The young nation was still pushing westward. Explorers and trappers had crossed the Mississippi River into virgin territory. Having heard glowing accounts of this new territory, Boone immigrated in October 1797 to what is now Missouri. It was then known as Upper Louisiana, an area controlled by Spain.

Daniel Boone's fame had come West ahead of him. On his arrival in St. Louis, he was met by the governor of the territory, who gave him land for a new home about 45 miles west of St. Louis, now St. Charles.

In July 1800 Boone was commissioned commandant of the Femme Osage district. His duties were both civil and military, and he fulfilled them with honor until the government purchased the territory from Spain in 1803.

Daniel Boone enjoyed his later years in Missouri. Many friends and many famous people visited him, as he himself was a famous person. He hunted and trapped in peace and wandered alone in the woods—things he had always enjoyed.

Then, for a second time, it seemed that he was going to lose everything. It was found that he did not have a clear title to his land, granted to him by Spain, but later purchased by the government. But Boone's friends in the

legislature interceded for him, and on the day before his 80th birthday, a bill confirming his title was passed.

In the meantime, Boone's wife of nearly 60 years had passed away in March 1813, at the age of 76. From now on, Boone made his home with his children, living to see his descendants of the fifth generation. No longer able to roam alone in the woods, he spent his time making powder horns and repairing rifles, since he was an expert at both.

In September 1820 Boone fell ill with fever while visiting his son, Major Nathan Boone. After an illness of three days, he died on September 26, 1820, in the 86th year of his life.

It is a remarkable fact that Daniel Boone was never wounded in his many fights with Indians. It seemed that he had a charmed life and was destined to enjoy a long lifetime of accomplishments as a frontiersman, explorer, founder of the State of Kentucky, and a leader of men.

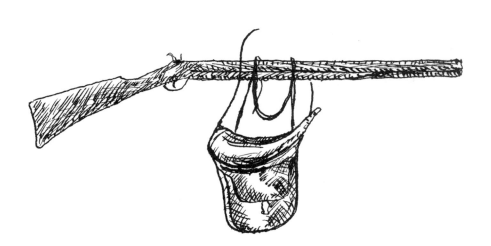

William Clark

1770-1838

Meriwether Lewis

1774-1809

II
William Clark
1770–1838

Meriwether Lewis
1774–1809

Before Thomas Jefferson was elected President in March 1801, he had envisioned making the vast, unknown country west of the Missouri river part of the United States. Two regular army officers, William Clark and Meriwether Lewis, were given the task of exploring and mapping this huge territory, which later became the westernmost boundary of the United States.

William Clark was born in Caroline County, Virginia, on August 1, 1770. His parents were John and Ann Clark. William was the youngest of a large family of six boys and four girls. Except for William, who was too young, all the boys served in the Revolutionary War. Four became general officers, and the second son, General George Rogers Clark, was a famous Revolutionary War hero and explorer.

Meriwether Lewis was born on August 18, 1774, the second child of William and Lucy Lewis, wealthy slave and landowners. Meriwether lived on the "Locust Hill" plantation about seven miles west of Charlottesville, Virginia, with his parents and an older sister and younger brother. His father died when he was five, and, when his mother remarried, the family moved to Georgia. But young Meriwether soon returned to Virginia to live with relatives. Since he was the child of a wealthy family, Meriwether received the best education the young country could provide. He both attended school and had private tutors. By contrast, William Clark probably had little formal education.

It is not certain when or how William Clark and Meriwether Lewis first met. But there were few families in Virginia at this time, and so they probably met early in life. Another Virginian, Thomas Jefferson, knew both families, and this acquaintance was to become important to both boys.

In the early 1790's, nearly ten years after the Revolutionary War, the young nation was still plagued by warfare with the British, the Indians, and the Spanish. William Clark joined the army in May 1791 and fought in a campaign against the British and their Indian allies. He was quickly promoted to lieutenant and then to captain under General Anthony Wayne. In 1793 General Wayne moved into Indian territory along the Ohio River. There Clark found himself in many skirmishes with the Indians and the British, who still occupied several forts on American soil.

Meriwether Lewis had meanwhile joined the Virginia militia as an ensign (a term later changed to lieutenant). He later transferred from his unit and served for a time under Captain Clark. The two men fought together in a campaign to drive the British out of Fort Miamis, originally built in 1764, but rebuilt and garrisoned again in 1794.

Clark, who had been in ill health for some years, resigned his army commission on July 1, 1796. This was the last of Clark's adventures until the expedition of 1804.

In March 1803 President Jefferson asked Lewis to become his personal secretary. Lewis quickly journeyed to Washington to accept this very important post. Soon Jefferson laid before Congress a plan for exploring the Louisiana Territory, which extended roughly from New Orleans up the Mississippi, Ohio, and Missouri rivers, then west to California and the Pacific Ocean. This vast area had never been thoroughly explored or mapped. Yet it promised both great wealth and great problems.

Wealth, because of its furs, timber, minerals, and other resources. Problems, because France laid claim to parts of it and the British might try to gain a foothold there as well, possibly causing another war. Jefferson had no way of knowing that he would soon be given the opportunity to purchase all of the Louisiana Territory.

There had been earlier territorial exploration. The Spaniards in 1540-42 had marched north, possibly as far as Kansas. In 1720 France sent a Jesuit father, who had partially studied routes to the Pacific. And a Jacques d'Eglise had paddled up the Missouri in 1790. But, since no records or maps were made by these early explorers, they are not considered predecessors of Lewis and Clark.

After receiving approval from Congress to pay $2,000,-000 for New Orleans, President Jefferson instructed his minister to France to see if that part of the Louisiana Territory could be purchased. But, since Napoleon, emperor of France, needed money to pay claims against France, he offered to sell the entire Louisiana Territory for $15,000,000. The bargain was immediately approved, and on October 19, 1803, Congress ratified the treaty. The next day President Jefferson instructed Meriwether Lewis, who had been planning the proposed expedition for months, to start selecting men and equipment. The expedition would be traveling through American territory that no known American had ever seen.

Meriwether Lewis was to be the leader of the expedition. He wanted to be accompanied by his friend William Clark, and, at Lewis's request, it was decided that the two men would have equal authority and act as co-leaders. First he needed Clark's acceptance. Lewis wrote from Washington on June 19, 1803, explaining that the expedition would explore both the Missouri and Columbia river valleys, then go on to the Pacific coast, and possibly return by sea on one of the vessels that put into the mouth of the Columbia to trade with Indians. Clark accepted at once.

Now began the task of recruiting men, buying guns, ammunition, and scientific instruments. The expedition had many commissions to perform. While Lewis was gathering equipment, and building boats, Clark was in Ohio and Kentucky recruiting men. Lewis and a party of men left Washington with the supplies on July 4, 1803, traveling by way of Harpers Ferry and Pittsburgh, then down the Ohio River. At last, on October 26, 1803, he joined Clark at Louisville, Kentucky. The journey now continued up the Ohio and the Mississippi. They paused for a time at Cape Girardeau, Missouri, and went into winter camp at Riviere du Bois on the Mississippi. They spent the winter recruiting new men and training them in the work to come.

Since this was an expedition under army orders, all civilians were now formally enlisted. The party, possibly less than 50 men, was divided into three squads with a sergeant in command of each and a regular army man named Ordway acting as a first sergeant. Lewis still held his army rank as a captain. He had asked the War Department to reinstate Clark to his old rank, but the department would not consider this. They did, however, give Clark the rank of lieutenant. This was not to Clark's liking, but as agreed earlier, Clark served the expedition as a "captain" with the same authority as Lewis.

The Lewis and Clark Expedition, sometimes known as the "Corps of Discovery," began its journey on Sunday, May 13, 1804. The expedition left camp at Riviere du Bois under the command of William Clark. Meriwether Lewis had gone ahead to St. Louis on business. Lewis joined the expedition when it reached St. Louis the next day. As noted in their reports, May 14 was the official start of the expedition under the joint command of Lewis and Clark.

The men and equipment were carried in three vessels: a 22-oar keelboat, or bateau; a large piragua; and a smaller pirogue. As with all such expeditions, several days passed before the men became used to handling the boats and equipment. Progress was slow, hard, and dangerous. When possible, some of the men walked or traveled on horseback along the river bank while others paddled or poled the boats. Both methods were difficult at times, because sheer cliffs rose from the river's banks, and the current below was swift, concealing many hazardous snags. At night the boats were tied up along the bank and camp was made on land.

At the start the expedition met other boats and rafts, manned by the hunters and trappers of the area. But as the men traveled further west, they saw only an occasional trader or Indians.

The expedition passed through the hunting grounds of the Oto, Osage, Pawnee, Omaha, Sioux, Missouri, Arikara, and lesser tribes. As each was met, Lewis tried to explain to the chiefs how and why they, as explorers, were there. The expedition had very little trouble with most of the lesser tribes, but always found itself in difficulty with the Sioux.

In late October the expedition built winter quarters on the left bank of the Missouri river, in the land of the Mandan Indians, north of what is now Bismarck, North Dakota. In April 1805 a party of soldiers left the expedition to return to Washington with the curios and natural history specimens that had been collected and to deliver Lewis's notes and reports to President Jefferson. Lewis, Clark, and the rest of the men resumed their westward journey to the coast.

Travel was both slow and treacherous as the country was rough and the river deep and dangerous. Although

game was plentiful, the Indians seemed to have abandoned the country.

From the beginning Lewis and Clark had planned to follow the Missouri as far west as possible, since it was thought that it reached almost to the Columbia River. But as they pushed westward, less and less was known of the course of the Missouri.

About 50 miles northeast of what is now Great Falls, Montana, the Missouri divides in two, one fork running north, one running south. When the expedition reached this point early in June, no one knew which fork should be followed. For days parties tracked the two forks without learning anything definite. Then Clark decided—correctly—that the south fork was the Missouri. The north fork they named Maria's River.

On June 11 Lewis and several of the men started along the bank of the river on foot, while Clark followed with the boats. On the third day out Lewis discovered the Great Falls of the Missouri and three days later was joined by Clark and the others. It was clear that they would have to portage around the rapids and smaller falls, a distance of about 16 miles. This meant leaving the larger boats and constructing wagons for the equipment. Those 16 miles cost them a full month of labor.

In late July the expedition reached the point where the Missouri ends in the Three Forks. The Missouri River so far had been their guide; it was now impossible to cross the Rockies without someone who knew the trails. Some months earlier, Lewis had hired a man named Charbonneau as an interpreter. Charbonneau was a "squaw-man," a white man who had married an Indian and lived with her tribe. His wife was Sacagawea, a girl of the Snake, or Shoshone tribe. As a baby, she had been captured and raised by the Minnetaree Indians. Much credit is given to this Indian girl for the success of the Lewis and Clark Expedition.

As Sacagawea began to recognize the country through which they were passing, they knew they were on the right track and in Shoshone territory. But before leaving

Three Forks, Lewis and Clark paused to name them: Jefferson's, Madison's, and Gallatin's rivers.

On July 30 the expedition continued the journey, and the success or failure of the Lewis and Clark Expedition now depended on locating the Shoshone Tribe to obtain both an Indian guide and horses. Time was growing short. Soon autumn would bring snow, and they must get across the mountains before winter or all would be lost. The Shoshones lived in the mountains and were a weak and timid tribe. When their scouts saw the expedition approaching, they were afraid and hid. After days of trying to make contact, Lewis encountered a small party of Shoshones on the trail. When the Shoshones met Sacagawea, one of their tribe, they became friendly. Lewis continued with his men and the Indians to their camp and on the way traveled up and over the Continental Divide.

While Lewis and his men were resting at the Shoshone camp, Clark and the rest of the party were toiling up river with the boats to reach the rendezvous point at the

forks of Jefferson's River. Lewis, after purchasing several horses from the Shoshone and arranging for a guide, started out from the Indian camp to meet up with Clark. On August 17 the party was reunited, and the success of the Lewis and Clark Expedition was assured.

Returning to the Shoshone camp, Lewis bought more horses, and the entire party made ready for the overland journey that was the last leg of their long, dangerous, and tiresome trip to the coast. On August 30 they left from the Shoshones, traveling with 29 horses and several Indian guides. Traveling along the Bitterroot River over the Lolo Trail into the land of the Flathead Indians, the expedition continued on its slow, wearisome, and hazardous way. In late September Clark, hunting for food ahead of the main party, sent back word that he had reached the North Fork of the Clearwater, a branch of the Columbia River, and was in touch with the friendly Nez Perce Indians. The expedition had crossed the Rockies!

Camp was made on the bank of the Clearwater River, and the party rested for a few days. Food was plentiful; game, fish, and other necessities could be traded with the Nez Perces. The horses were left with the Indians and canoes built to continue the journey by water to the Pacific. On October 16 the expedition reached the main stream of the Columbia, and a few days later they saw in the distance Mt. Adams and Mt. Hood. They soon reached the lower Columbia, meeting a few English-speaking Indians who had had contact with sailors who had rounded Cape Horn. In another few days, on November 14, they reached their goal: the Pacific Ocean.

The expedition now went into camp, but wind and rain forced them to look for a more suitable site. Lewis and Clark realized they would have to winter on the coast. They had planned—and still hoped—to return with a trading vessel instead of overland. A site was soon found, and by mid-December the cabins, storerooms, and stables, now named Fort Clatsop, were completed. There was plenty of work to be done. As the men hunted for food and repaired clothing and equipment, Lewis worked over his notes of the botanical and zoological features of the regions they had passed through, while Clark completed his maps and topographical data.

It was decided that they would have to make an early start if they wanted to get home before the end of 1806. As spring approached, all hope was abandoned for a ship to transport them home. The expedition broke camp, and the return journey began on March 23. The expedition traveled back up the Columbia River, crossing the Rockies only with the help of the Nez Perces and the Shoshones, since the passes were still filled with snow. Reaching the banks of the Clearwater River in late April, they were able to find supplies that they had cached on their way to the coast. The journey back was hard and dangerous, but knowing what they were up against helped.

In June the expedition journeyed back over the Lolo Trail, through the Bitterroot range. At last, on July 3, the time had come for the "Corps of Discovery" to split up. There were still vast areas of unknown country to explore north and south of their westward route. It was decided that Lewis would lead a party overland north of the Missouri, while Clark and the others would go south to the Yellowstone River and float down into the Missouri. The two parties would meet at the junction of the two rivers.

Lewis and party reached the Great Falls on July 13, and, traveling through the territory of the warlike Blackfeet, later arrived at Maria's River. One day Lewis was accidentally shot by one of his own hunting party. Although the wound was not serious, it caused him much pain.

Clark meanwhile had traveled down Jefferson's River to the Yellowstone. On August 11 he made his first contact with civilization: two white trappers.

Lewis soon reached the bluffs overhanging the Missouri, and each day he kept a sharp lookout for Clark. Later, passing the mouth of the Yellowstone, a note was found saying that Clark was camped only a few days down river.

On August 13 the two leaders and their men were reunited. Heading east again, now among friendly Mandan Indians, where there was plenty of buffalo for food and clothing, they came to the Mandan villages. Here the expedition began to disband. Some of the men were eager to leave immediately for their homes, others headed into the mountains to trap fur. Sacagawea and her husband were home. Much of what little equipment and supplies remained was given to the men and Indians.

All who remained with the expedition went on to St. Joseph, then to St. Charles. After spending a few days at Fort Bellefontaine, they passed their old camp at Riviere de Bois. By noon on September 23 they reached St. Louis and the end of their journey, all with the loss of only one man, a Sergeant Floyd who had died of illness on their way out to the coast.

The entire country rejoiced over the safe return of the Lewis and Clark Expedition. The 32 men had been gone for more than two years and no word had been received from them. Many had given up hope that any of the party

would return alive. The men were now paid off: besides his soldier's pay, each received 320 acres of government land. Lewis and Clark each received 1,600 acres and $1,228 in pay.

Both leaders, anxious to join their families, started east, reaching Louisville in November. Here they parted. Lewis went on to Washington to give his report to President Jefferson. Clark returned to Virginia.

Meriwether Lewis arrived in Washington early in January and for a time was the outstanding figure in the nation's capital. As the governorship of the Louisiana territory was vacant, he was offered this post, accepted it, and took office early in 1807. Political tasks were new to the explorer, and these, combined with his family's financial affairs, caused him much anxiety. Many times he wished he had not accepted the governorship. As things grew worse both in his public and private life, Meriwether Lewis grew more unhappy. Men within his political party were working against him. Many of his business ventures failed; and the federal government would not honor the vouchers he had had to issue for government claims. During the summer of 1809, things were growing worse and more irritating. Jefferson had retired to private life, and President Madison would not help. Lewis decided he would have to visit Washington to present his claims in person.

Lewis, at this time in very poor health, left St. Louis on September 4, 1809, traveling down the Mississippi to New Orleans, then by coach and horseback overland through Tennessee. He stopped off for a few days at Chickasaw Bluffs (Memphis), and then with a small party struck out through Indian country along the Natchez Trace, a narrow wilderness road that ran from Natchez to Nashville. Lewis never reached Nashville.

While on the Trace, the party stopped for the night at a rest camp, Grinder's Stand. Lewis, ill (and according to some accounts deranged in mind) either committed suicide or was murdered by a person or persons unknown. It has never been proved whether it was suicide or murder. But, considering Lewis's unhappy state of mind, suicide seems the more likely. At the early age of 35 on October 11, 1809, explorer Meriwether Lewis died.

William Clark, after his return east, had been made a brigadier general of Louisiana Militia. There was still trouble with Indian tribes, and it was Clark's duty to keep them confined to the territory agreed to by treaty. Clark, too, had his problems with those in government—mainly because of his friendship with Lewis rather than through any fault of his own.

Clark was in Kentucky when the news of Lewis's death reached him. He immediately took charge of his friend's affairs. As Lewis had never married, Lewis's scant possessions were willed to his mother.

William Clark was now made governor of the territory and superintendent of Indian Affairs and later found himself acting as both governor and Indian fighter as the War of 1812 approached.

Clark's early friendship with many Indian chiefs during the Lewis and Clark Expedition was the deciding factor in negotiating an Indian treaty and bringing peace to the territory in 1825. Unlike Lewis, Clark was a success as territorial governor. Nevertheless, he later refused to run for re-election, although he continued as superintendent of Indian Affairs until 1821.

In his later years Clark lived well. He had invested successfully in land and was considered a wealthy man. His home was always open to friends and Indian chiefs, who visited him on many occasions. Married twice, Clark outlived both wives. He moved in with a favorite son, Meriwether Lewis Clark, and at the age of 68, on September 1, 1838, William Clark died peacefully.

David Crockett

1786-1836

III

David Crockett

1786–1836

Frontiersman, farmer, soldier, and statesman was the legendary hero David (Davy) Crockett. He was born August 17, 1786. His parents, Joseph and Rebecca Hawkins Crockett, lived along the banks of the Nolachucky River in what is now Hawkins County, Tennessee.

Joseph Crockett, a native of Ireland, had fought bravely in the Revolutionary War. When the war ended, he emigrated to Tennessee, married, and raised several children. The family home was in a wild and sparsely settled part of the country, and farming was difficult due to Indian attack upon the settlers. Finally, to give Davy and the other children an opportunity for an education, the father moved near the small settlement of Greenville and opened a tavern.

The Crockett tavern became the stopping-off place for many travelers, and it was from these people Davy received most of his early education. He was quick to learn the ways of the wilderness from those around him. When he was eight years old, his father gave him a rifle but allowed him only one load a day. His father warned him that any evening he came home without game he would get no supper. Small wonder Davy soon became an expert marksman!

When Davy was 12, he and his brothers were enrolled in a private school that had been founded nearby. Davy's brothers soon accepted their new roles as students. But not Davy. After a few days shut up in a small room with books, Davy was ready to rebel. A fight with another student and a disagreement over this with his father put an end to his elementary education.

As Davy would not go to school, his father decided he should go to work. While still only 12, Davy hired out to a neighbor to help move a drove of cattle to Port Royal, Virginia, five or six hundred miles away. This should have frightened so young a boy. But not Davy Crockett. On his way home after being paid off at Port Royal, Davy met a wagoner delivering goods to Gerardstown, near Winchester. His desire to travel was greater than his homesickness, so he joined this man.

After reaching Gerardstown, he hired out to a farmer for several months until he had saved enough money to travel onward. He finally visited Baltimore to take in the sights of a large city. Davy soon found himself along the waterfront and was awed by the ships that were tied up at the wharf. He decided to become a sailor and see that strange world beyond the seas. He at once applied to the captain of one of the ships for a job and was hired. But when he went to get his clothes, the man he was staying with refused to let him join the ship's crew. He knew that Davy was too young to be happy with such a life and soon convinced him that someone raised as a hunter in the wilderness would not make a very good sailor.

Davy, now penniless, soon started to work his way back to Tennessee. He worked as a wagoner, as a farm hand, as an apprentice to a hatter, and at several other jobs; in fact, any that offered pay, until finally he had enough money to return home. Davy Crockett had now been away for three years: his parents and brothers and sisters hardly recognized him.

Finding his father in debt, Davy gave him his savings and hired out with a neighbor until there was enough money to pay off the debts. Davy, now 16, decided it was time to learn to read and write. For six months he worked two days and went to school four days. Aside from the

JAMES L. VLASA

few days he had spent in school at the age of 12, this was the only formal education David Crockett, the future statesman from Tennessee, ever had.

At 18 David Crockett married. His bride's parents gave them two cows and a calf and a man Davy had once worked for gave them 15 dollars. The couple rented a small farm; but rent payments and poor crops made it impossible for them to support a family. With Davy's father-in-law they moved to another small farm in Franklin County, Tennessee.

As the War of 1812 approached, the settlers found themselves in constant danger of Indian attacks. Davy Crockett fought many skirmishes with Indians; he was an expert rifleman and possessed a natural shrewdness in dealing with the warriors. At times he was made leader over small groups of men sent to scout enemy forces. Later he served under the command of General Andrew (Old Hickory) Jackson.

A treaty was signed in 1814 bringing the war to an end, and David Crockett returned to farming and hunting in Franklin County. It was during this time that his wife suddenly fell ill and died, leaving him with three small children. Davy realized he could not give his children the care they needed and soon married a widow with two children and started another life with a new family.

Some months later he set out with three men to explore new territory. A few weeks later he fell ill with fever and for weeks lingered between life and death. When he was well enough to travel again, he turned back. A few months later Davy decided to move his family about 80 miles to Shoals Creek, land recently bought from the Indians. There the Crockett family started building a new home and life. As Davy was not fond of the hard life of a farmer, he decided to go into business; when the cabin was completed, he built a distillery and a small mill for grinding grain.

Several families lived at Shoals Creek, and soon a township was formed. Crockett was chosen magistrate. Later an election was held for military ranks in a regiment being formed. Crockett hoped to become a major, but due to his past record as an Indian fighter, his humor and honesty, and his standing among the settlers in this small community, he won the higher rank of colonel.

His rise in the military and in civil government did not stop here. He was elected to the state legislature in 1821. David Crockett was not an educated man, having had less than a year's schooling, but due to his extensive travels as a boy, his quickness of mind, and his fairness in judgment, he was now and in later years always well-liked and judged to be an able man for any job.

In 1822 misfortune struck again when all his holdings —the cabins, mill, and distillery—were swept away in a flood. All other possessions had to be sold to pay off creditors. Once again, David Crockett was penniless. Taking his family to another location along the Albion River, he built a new cabin and cleared the land for cultivation. Since providing for his family now took up all his time, he resigned from political life.

In the spring of 1823, Davy Crockett visited the nearby trading post of Jackson. Here he encountered several old war comrades who prevailed upon him to run again for the legislature. He declined, but his name was put before the people, and once again he was elected.

It was during this term in office that Crockett made an enemy of a man who was to become President. He voted against his old commander, General Andrew Jackson, for U.S. senator because he did not consider Jackson qualified for the position. Crockett and Jackson were destined to be at odds for the rest of Crockett's life.

In 1824 the people insisted upon Davy running for the U.S. Congress; he did, and, for the first time in his life, was defeated.

For the next two years David Crockett kept away from politics, worked his small farm, hunted, and trapped. On one occasion he built two large flatboats and loaded them with furs, meat, and other products to take to New Orleans. But Davy Crockett was destined not to succeed in any business venture. After reaching the Mississippi, neither he nor his men were able to navigate. They ran aground on an island, the swift river current sank the boats, and the men barely escaped with their lives.

In 1826 it was time for another congressional election. Davy decided to try for office again, and his many friends donated money for his campaign. There were those who thought Crockett had no chance of beating his strong opponent, but when the votes were counted, Colonel Crockett became Congressman Crockett.

Davy Crockett was one of the most outstanding congressmen. He favored the administration during his first two years, but later differed with Jackson (now President Jackson) on many policies. Jackson and the party opposed Crockett, but he was again re-elected in 1829. When he ran for a third term, few thought he could win over all the wealth and influence pitted against him, but he was re-elected by a small majority.

Colonel David Crockett was known from the Atlantic to the Mississippi for his opposition to President Jackson, who was unpopular with many people, and for his original and sometimes humorous speeches on the floor of Congress. As he traveled the East, he was amazed at the crowds of people anxious to see and meet him. He was called upon time and time again to meet with distinguished citizens and to give talks; he had a style and delivery that delighted all. In Boston his portrait was painted. In Philadelphia the young Whigs of the city presented him with a beautiful rifle. This rifle, which he named "Old Betsy," was among his most cherished possessions.

After this successful tour of the large cities along the coast, Davy Crockett returned to his duties in Washington. Soon the business of the House was finished and Crockett left Washington, little dreaming that this would be his last trip there as a congressman. At the next election David Crockett was beaten. In his first bid for office, he had cared little whether he won or lost; but now being beaten after three successful terms in Congress meant his hopes for fame and glory were gone. Davy blamed his defeat on Andrew Jackson, the man and the President with whom he had so openly differed many, many times.

After this last congressional defeat his political career was finished. For the next few years he farmed and attempted several small business ventures, none of which made him a rich man. In 1835 Davy Crockett, still holding his military rank of colonel, took leave of his family and started for the West. He planned to visit the southwest, now the scene of conflict between Texas and Mexico. There, in the victory of battle, he hoped to win back the fame he had lost in the votes of an election. He made his way down the Mississippi and on to Little Rock, Arkansas, where he spent some time with old friends. Davy traveled on to Greenville, then to Fulton, Missouri, on by steamboat and by horseback. After several weeks of slow and difficult travel, he reached his destination in Texas—the fortress of Alamo.

Davy Crockett was warmly welcomed by Colonel Travis, the commander of the 150 defenders of the Alamo. Three days later the Army of Mexico, 5,000 men led by General Santa Anna, attacked the Alamo but could not penetrate its walls. Finally, after 11 days of siege, the Alamo was attacked by the entire Mexican command. Soon it was over—one of the bloodiest hand-to-hand conflicts in American history. There were few survivors: women and children, families of the defenders.

Colonel David Crockett, frontiersman, farmer, soldier, and statesman, at the age of fifty was killed in the line of duty, but his defense of the Alamo is immortalized in American history.

Samuel Houston

1793-1863

IV
Samuel Houston
1793–1863

Samuel Houston of Texas, hero of San Jacinto, was one of the most independent, unique, popular, hated, forceful, and dramatic individuals ever to serve his country. At 14 he became the adopted son of a Cherokee chief; at 27, after six years in the army, attorney general of Nashville; at 33, governor of Tennessee; founder and president of the Republic of Texas; then senator from Texas; and later twice elected governor of the new state of Texas. That was Sam Houston.

Sam Houston was born on March 2, 1793, at the family plantation, Timber Ridge, on the main road to Lexington, Kentucky. Sam was the fifth of nine children born to Samuel and Elizabeth Houston.

Sam was a poor student and a truant. He preferred to hunt in the woods, swim in the creek, or ride through the countryside on horseback. Although he disliked school, he was fond of books and spent many hours in his father's library. One could say in later years that Sam Houston was a self-educated man.

Sam's father did not care for farming. He preferred the easy life of a military officer. When Sam was 13, his father, then 50 and in poor health, was forced to resign his commission. He sold the plantation to settle debts, and a few months later he died, leaving the family bankrupt.

Sam's mother gathered the remnants of her once proud and wealthy family and set out for Tennessee. She settled the family on a homestead of 419 acres at Baker's Creek, near Maryville.

Sam, now 14, was expected to share in the work, but his inclinations did not include clearing land and farming. He was the handsomest of all the boys and well-liked, but lazy. He would disappear for days in the woods, usually with a book. Finally the family agreed that Sam would never be a farmer, and he was sent to Maryville to work as a clerk. But clerking suited Sam Houston no better than farming. He disappeared, and, several weeks later, searchers found him living with the Cherokee Indians.

Sam lived with his Indian family for several years. This was the life he had always wanted; the young braves taught him their dances and their games, and he could roam the woods freely and observe the wild life. Chief Oolooteka adopted Sam as a son and christened him Colonneh—the Raven.

Young Sam bought powder and shot on credit for his Indian friends, and by the time he was 19, he owed $100. He returned to Maryville to take a job. Jobs were scarce, so he decided to open a private school. This announcement was greeted with laughter, but Sam made a success of the school, and his debt was paid. For the first time in his life, Sam Houston had money in his pocket that he had earned.

The following year Sam entered military service in the War of 1812. He was soon commissioned an ensign. In February, 1814, Ensign Houston and the 39th Infantry marched into Fort Strother to serve under General Andrew Jackson. In a battle with the Creek Indians, Ensign Houston led a charge in which he was seriously wounded; first by an arrow in his thigh and later by two bullets; one shattered his right arm and another smashed his right shoulder.

Without medical attention it was only due to Sam's strength and will to survive that he did not die from his wounds. Two months after the battle, Sam reached home,

where, nursed by his mother, he recovered. Early in 1815 Sam rejoined his regiment in Tennessee. Army doctors removed the bullet from his shoulder, but the operation was so severe that he was lamed for life. He was promoted to second lieutenant and transferred to New Orleans, and then to Nashville for duty with the Southern Division of the Army, again serving under Andrew Jackson. The following year Sam requested a transfer, which Jackson endorsed, and he became Indian agent for the Cherokee Nation. He wanted this post to make sure that his Indian brothers got the rights they had been granted by treaties.

When Lieutenant Houston left the army, he sold his interest in Baker's Creek homestead to pay off his debts and once again found himself out of money and out of a job. He went to Nashville and in the law office of James Trimble began to read law; in six months he astonished all by passing the examination for admission to the bar. Sam now went to Lebanon, 30 miles from Nashville, to practice and was an instant success both as a lawyer and with the social element of this small frontier community. Soon, due to this success and his friendship with Andrew Jackson and Governor McMinn, Sam Houston was appointed adjutant general of the state militia. This made him Colonel Houston.

Colonel Sam Houston rose rapidly in politics. He was elected attorney general of the Nashville district but later resigned to enter private law practice with its larger rewards. He became the right-hand man of the new Governor, William Carroll, who at this time was promoting Andrew Jackson for the coming Presidency. In 1823 with

the help of Jackson and Governor Carroll, Sam Houston was nominated for Congress, and with no opposition received every vote cast.

Five years before, Sam Houston had left Washington City a disillusioned ex-lieutenant without occupation or prospects; now he was to return as a major general, a congressman-elect, and protégé of the most popular man in the country, Andrew Jackson. Sam was now just 30 years of age.

In 1824 Sam Houston went back home to Nashville and was re-elected to Congress. He began to show his leadership in Congress during his second term, but in doing so made enemies.

Andrew Jackson now proposed Sam Houston to succeed the retiring William Carroll as governor of Tennessee. Sam Houston wanted the office and conducted a vigorous campaign. When the votes were counted, Samuel Houston, the favorite son of the people of Tennessee, was elected governor at the age of 33.

Sam served his people with justice and knowledge of frontier conditions. On January 22, 1829, at the age of 35, he surprised his friends by getting married. As Sam and his 18-year-old bride, Eliza Allen, had no home, they moved to the Nashville Inn, where Sam lived and conducted the affairs of governor.

Then, three months later, Sam's young wife suddenly left him and went home. Sam, then running for re-election, gave up the campaign and in a few days left Nashville.

No one knows why Sam and his wife parted, but this separation was a tragic episode in his life and the deciding factor in much of what was to follow. After leaving Nashville, Sam traveled by steamboat to Memphis, then on to Little Rock. At Webbers' Falls, headquarters of the new Cherokee Nation, Sam was received by Chief Oolooteka, his foster father.

Sam's return was welcomed by his Indian friends. The Cherokees, like all Indian tribes, had been moved from territory to territory by the government and cheated by

Indian agents. They had no food, no money, no land for crops or hunting. The Raven's coming, after an absence of many years, was looked on as a good omen. Sam, too, was aware of their trouble and knew of the treaties that had been broken. Chief Oolooteka had visions of uniting all the eastern tribes and moving west to fight the Comanches and Pawnees and take over their lands. Sam Houston did not want an Indian war, knowing that all tribes would lose in the end.

On January 13, 1830, Sam and a representative of the Cherokee Nation called upon President Andrew Jackson to work out a peaceful solution. Jackson was disappointed that his long-time friend had given up politics, but agreed with Sam on the Indian problem.

In May, Sam returned to the Cherokees and took a half-breed woman named Tiana Rogers as a wife. Sam's political enemies stopped his plans again and again in the years that followed. Sam tried his hand as a trader, but he could not get a license from the government. All his requests for help for his Indian friends were rejected. Sam turned to drink and his Indian friends gave him a new name, Ootsetee Ardeetahskee, meaning "Big Drunk."

In September 1831 Sam was called home to his mother's bedside at Baker's Creek. She died a few hours after he arrived. In October Sam was back with the Cherokees sitting with them in council—but as the Raven, not Ootsetee Ardeetahskee. Sam Houston had once again found himself. Now, at the age of 39, a new phase began to take shape in his life.

The status of Texas had been in doubt for some time. Although originally a part of the Louisiana Purchase, Texas had been retained by Spain. Then, after winning its independence from Spain, Mexico claimed Texas. Mexico's claim to Texas was disputed by many Americans, including Sam Houston, who had visions of "doing something grand—to capture an empire and lay it at the feet of his old friend," President Jackson. On December 1, 1832, Sam was at Fort Towson on the American bank of the Red River. The next day he mounted his horse and

crossed the river into Texas, beginning a new epoch in the history of Texas and in the heroic life of Samuel Houston.

As the envoy of President Jackson, he rode south to Nacogdoches and on to San Felipe de Austin to consult with Stephen Austin, one of the leaders working for Texas independence. Later Sam met another famous frontiersman, Jim Bowie, who had come to Texas from Georgia. A few weeks later Sam and others received word that General Santa Anna would be sworn in as president of Mexico on April 1, 1833. It was decided that Santa Anna should be requested to grant Texas independence from Mexico. General Sam Houston — now known as Don Samuel de Houston—was a delegate from Nacogdoches to a convention to draft the formal request to the Mexican government.

Sam Houston spent days and weeks traveling and working in behalf of independence. To further his interests, Sam opened a law practice in Nacogdoches and represented not only important clients but the Galveston Bay and Texas Land Company as well. As the months passed, it became clear that President Santa Anna was not going to consent to the independence of Texas.

In the fall of 1834, Sam Houston was in Washington to confer with President Jackson over the Texas question. He had previously written Jackson that "the people of Texas are determined to form a State Government—free themselves from Mexico—and if the United States will not accept the territory as a new State of the Union, then Texas must and will adopt a transfer to some other power." Houston returned to Texas and in the autumn of 1835, acting as Commander of the Armies of Texas Republic, set about recruiting volunteers for the Texas Revolution.

Seeing that a battle was soon to take place, Santa Anna sent his brother-in-law, Martin Perfecto Cos, to command the Mexican army in Texas, headquartered at San Antonio de Bexar. But General Houston did not want to meet the Mexican army yet. He felt that the volunteer American army, under the command of Stephen Austin, was not yet strong enough to win. Then, without Houston's order, 300 American volunteers stormed the garrison of General Cos; 1,400 Mexican soldiers surrendered and were permitted to march back into Mexico. There was not now a Mexican soldier north of the Rio Grande.

But Sam Houston's dream for an "empire of Texas" was not to come so easily. General Santa Anna soon marched north with 5,000 men to avenge the victory of the Americans at San Antonio de Bexar and regain Texas. On March 6, 1836, he attacked and overwhelmed the Alamo. He then marched toward Gonzales, held by Houston and 800 men. Houston, realizing that he could not make a stand, hoping to join forces with the 390 men under Colonel James Fannin, ordered a retreat.

During the retreat, Houston got word that Fannin's men had been captured and executed by Santa Anna. Houston now had no choice; if Texas was to gain independence, he would have to face the Mexican Army. Santa Anna went into camp with an army of 1,350 men near Lynch's Ferry on the Rio San Jacinto. The date was April 21, 1836. Houston decided to attack, and at 3:30 o'clock in the afternoon (a time that no army commander would ever attack, or think of being attacked), the ragged, underfed, and underpaid "volunteers" of Sam Houston overran the camp of Santa Anna's men. In a furious 20-minute, hand-to-hand combat, they routed the Mexican regulars with the battle cry, "Remember the Alamo!" General Santa Anna was captured, and the Mexican claim to Texas was settled.

General Houston had been severely wounded in the battle, and it was thought he could not live. He was brought to New Orleans, where surgeons removed 20 pieces of bone from the wound in his leg. Only his reserve strength and will power kept Sam Houston alive.

The Republic of Texas, now free from Mexico, was in a sad state. On July 5 Houston returned to San Augustine, the capital, and found it in a state of confusion. David G. Burnet had been elected provisional president some

months earlier, but both he and his cabinet proved to be incompetent. Burnet now realized he could not govern Texas. In the general election called for September 5, 1836, Sam Houston was elected president of the Republic of Texas.

It had always been Sam Houston's dream that, after Texas gained independence, annexation by the United States would follow. President Jackson and many citizens favored this. But Northerners in Congress opposed it, knowing that Texas would be admitted as a slave state. While Congress delayed, President Houston had no funds for salaries or for the affairs of government. President Jackson did what he could, partially relieving the Republic's financial crisis on his last day in office by signing a bill of assistance.

The new Congress under President Houston convened at the capital (named after Sam Houston) on May 1, 1837. Their difficulties were enormous: very little money, no suitable buildings for government offices, people moving in without regular employment or homes, and, above all, the question of annexation. Andrew Jackson had been succeeded by Martin Van Buren who also favored Texas statehood.

At the expiration of his one-year term as President, Houston was replaced by his Vice-President, General Mirabeau Lamar, who did not favor annexation and who decided to change the Republic's capital to Austin, named for Stephen Austin.

Sam Houston now visited the United States seeking capital for his Texas enterprises. While in Mobile, he met a Margaret Lea, a young lady of 20, and again (as he had several times in the past) fell in love. On May 9, 1840, Sam Houston and Margaret Lea were married in Marion, Alabama. Sam was now 47, his bride 21.

The new Texas Republic was not prospering under President Lamar. Lamar had incited an Indian war in which Houston's foster-father, Oolooteka of the Cherokees, was slain. Texas was again bankrupt, and all of Lamar's schemes to create a new country had failed.

In the minds of the people, there was only one man to lead them out of chaos. On December 13, 1841, Sam Houston again assumed the presidency of the Republic and with it the debts and uncertainties of the Lamar administration. Again Houston was the capital.

In the fall of 1842, Mexico made another attempt to reclaim Texas. Santa Anna raided San Antonio in September, and Sam Houston again took to the field. Mexico soon came to terms, and again Texas was free. On the day of the signing of the truce, Sam Houston, Jr. was 10 weeks old.

By 1843 the Republic was functioning but still hoping for annexation by the United States. At the same time England and France wanted to annex Texas to gain a foothold in this part of the world. President John Tyler was trying to influence Congress to agree to annexation, but the northern segment resisted. Time passed, and a new head of state, James K. Polk, was President. He, too, was agreeable to annexation, but the Senate again rejected the proposal. Meanwhile, Sam Houston's term as president ran out. Under the Texas Constitution he could never be president again. He maneuvered the election of Anson Jones and then retired with his wife and son to their new home at Huntsville, "Raven Hill."

The United States began to realize that if they did not accept Texas, England would go to any lengths to annex the Republic. Northern opposition waned and on March 1, 1845, the treaty was signed. That vast land known as the Republic of Texas was now a part of the United States. Sam Houston thought his work was finished, but Texas still needed him. In March 1846 he took his place in the U.S. Senate.

Samuel Houston served well in the Senate, and he began to be thought of as a possible candidate for the Presidency. But the nation was split over the question of slavery. Texas had joined the Union as a slave state. Sam Houston, like many other southerners, was forced to choose between his loyalty to the Union and his loyalty to the South. Sam did not want to see the nation split into two countries, North and South. In a famous speech in the Senate, he expressed his loyalty to the Union of North and South, and in doing so lost the support of the people of Texas.

In August 1857 against the advice of friends and without resigning from the Senate, Houston ran for the governorship of Texas, but was defeated. In March 1859 when his term in the Senate ended, Sam Houston left Washington to return to Texas; he was never to leave it again.

But Sam Houston could not reconcile himself to being a private citizen. In 1859 he ran again for the governorship and was elected, assuming for the seventh time the affairs of government in Texas. In the crucial presidential election of 1860, Abraham Lincoln assumed the Presidency and the black years of the Civil War.

Against the wishes and advice of Governor Houston, Texas seceded from the Union on the side of the Confederacy on March 16, 1861. Texas supported the Confederacy by sending many men to battle—among them, Sam Houston, Jr., who was wounded at the battle of Shiloh Church in Tennessee. Houston spoke out many times against the war and in doing so lost many friends.

Houston's health was failing, and in 1862 he was expected to die of "consumption." But a few days later he regained his strength and moved with his family into the famous Steamboat House in Huntsville. His popularity increased, and when he visited Houston City in March 1863, he was asked to run again for the governorship. He declined on the grounds of uncertain health.

The end came suddenly. Sam Houston came home from Houston City ill with a cold and later contracted pneumonia. On July 26, 1863, he died peacefully in his sleep, surrounded by his family.

Sam Houston's mother had, 50 years before, given her son a plain, gold ring. Sam wore this ring during his lifetime. After death it was removed by his wife; on the inside was the inscription—a single word—"HONOR."

James Bowie

1796-1836

V
James Bowie
1796–1836

Jim Bowie, whose name calls up legends of duels, Indian fights, slave smuggling, land speculation, and exploits with the celebrated knife that bears his name, was another frontiersman who gave much of himself in settling the early West. Very little is known of Jim's childhood. His father, Rezin Bowie, a soldier of the Revolution, had been captured and imprisoned by the British at Savannah. There he met his future wife when she came to nurse the sick and wounded. After the war, the Bowie family moved constantly, living in Georgia, Tennessee, and Kentucky, where it is thought that Jim was born. They finally settled near Opelansas, not too many miles from New Orleans, Louisiana. Jim's father died suddenly after their arrival in Louisiana, and the six Bowie children were raised by their mother, Elve Bowie.

The Bowie boys were hard workers, but Jim always took the lead in any venture where money was concerned. At 19, more than six feet tall, strong, and physically equipped for the hard life of the frontier, Jim started farming on several acres near Bayou Boeuf. Within a year his homestead was one of the best in the area. Unhappily, a girl he was in love with married another, so he sold the farm and formed a partnership with his favorite older brother, Rezin. Pooling their money, they bought land in Bayou Lafourche country and started a sugar plantation. At that time there was more money in sugar than in any other crop. In two years, fields were in, buildings completed, and the brothers sold the holdings at a good price. Jim Bowie now realized that money was to be made in land speculation. The next few years were spent in buying land, clearing it, planting crops, and then selling out at a good profit. Jim and his brother became wealthy.

Jim, now 24, was joined by an old friend, Jess Leeman. It was from this older man that Jim learned the art of woodcraft and the use of the lariat and the knife. As his skill with knives grew, Jim began to feel that none of them had all the qualities he wanted. He eventually designed his own. The Bowie knife had a straight blade about nine inches long, sharpened on both sides, and a short guard to protect the handle. From Jess Leeman Jim also heard about Texas, a land just waiting for settlers to move in and stake out claims.

Jim was anxious to see it, so in 1819 he and Rezin traveled to Texas to the frontier settlement of Nacogdoches. At this time Spain still claimed Texas, but the settlers had proclaimed it a republic, independent of Spain. The settlers had formed a civil government with James Long as president.

When Jim and his brother arrived at Nacogdoches, they again encountered Jess Leeman, who had been hired by Long to guide an expedition to Campeachy. This was the stronghold of Jean Lafitte, a notorious pirate. Long hoped for Lafitte's help in driving the Spaniards from Texas. Jim was asked to go along and was delighted to do so, as it gave him the opportunity to explore the land.

The pirate leader Lafitte had built his stronghold on Galveston Island, where his ships could shelter. His trade was in slaves taken from ships he captured on their way from Africa to the New World. When the Long party reached the island, they saw hundreds of slaves in the "slavepens" waiting to be sold. Long could not persuade Lafitte to join forces with him, and the party returned to Nacogdoches. They found the town abandoned after being attacked by the Spaniards. Several more engagements with the Spaniards were fought, but Long's men were always outnumbered, and the cause was soon lost. Long and the remnants of his little army retreated to the Louisiana border.

Jim's only interest now was in becoming rich in as short a time as possible. Jim Bowie was a hard and ruthless man when it came to business. Seeing the hundreds of slaves being held for buyers at Lafitte's stronghold,

Bowie immediately saw an opportunity to make a lot of money. He and Rezin soon were in the business of buying and selling slaves. The slaves were bought from Lafitte, then smuggled into Louisiana and sold to the authorities as escaped slaves.

Jim and Rezin made more money from slave smuggling than they at first thought possible. They knew, however, that it was a risky business. Soon, having made a lot of quick and easy money, they returned to land investments in Louisiana. They bought 3,000 acres near Thibodauxville on Bayou Lafourche and began to improve it. When the plantation was finished, they named it Acadia. The house was copied after the mansions they had seen at Natchez, and when it and the other buildings were finished, they had the finest and most complete plantation in the area.

On one of Jim's river trips, he saw a paddle-wheel steamboat and was impressed by the engine that drove it. He later worked out a plan for the same type of engine to be used in the sugar mill at Acadia plantation. Jim Bowie is credited with giving Louisiana its first steam-operated sugar press. The plantation prospered, and soon the surrounding countryside was settled by people from other parts.

In 1825 Jim was involved in one of the incidents that made the Bowie knife a legend. A political feud had been brewing in the community for years and at last it led to a duel between two prominent settlers. The duel ended in a draw, but it was followed by a battle among the witnesses, among whom was Bowie. Jim killed a man with his knife, but he, too, nearly died of wounds.

In 1828 Jim's restlessness again brought him to Texas. He was sure that land in this part of the country was a good investment and would soon attract settlers. He was also sure that Mexico would eventually split from Spain and take Texas with it. Jim Bowie wanted to be there when grants of land were offered. Jim and Rezin traveled to San Felipe de Austin where they met Stephen Austin, one of the early colonizers of Texas. Austin put Jim in touch with the Veramendi family of San Antonio de Bexar. The head of the family, Don Juan Veramendi, was vice-governor of Texas and the territory's leading Mexican citizen.

Jim Bowie and Don Veramendi soon became close friends, realizing that they could help each other and Mexico as well in winning her independence. Jim soon made known his desire to accumulate land. But Texas colonists, such as Bowie, were not allowed to own more than one league of land—4,428.4 acres. With the backing of the Veramendis and other powerful families, Jim became a Mexican citizen. Now he could own 50,000 acres. With the assistance of influential friends, however, Bowie soon held options to almost a million acres of Texas land.

During this time Jim and one of the Veramendi daughters, Ursula, fell in love. On April 23, 1831, after the customary long Mexican courtship, Jim Bowie and Ursula de Veramendi were married. On their honeymoon they visited Jim's mother in Opelansas and had their portraits painted by John James Audubon in New Orleans.

This was a successful marriage, although Jim was constantly traveling in different business ventures. He was a born leader and his friends called him "Leoncito," the young lion. Jim and his young friends helped to keep down the raids by Comanche Indians on the haciendas. Once Jim, Rezin, seven men, and two servants left San Antonio early in November, 1832, to search for silver. In the San Saba country, they were attacked by a large party of Indians. After eight days of fighting, the Indians gave up. They had lost 82 men—and had killed only one of Jim's party and had wounded three others.

Trouble had been brewing in Texas for some time. Many Mexicans were afraid that unless the Americans were driven out, the United States would lay claim to the Texas territory. The government in Mexico City began to impose taxes on American landowners and in many cases refused to confirm title to their land. Jim Bowie, now a Mexican citizen, worked hard to help the American landowners keep their land and to avert a war.

But it was impossible to keep the settlers under control. William Barrett Travis, a West Point graduate, finally stirred the settlers to action. They stormed Fort Velasco at the mouth of the Brazos River, and, with the help of a gunboat anchored offshore, forced the surrender of the Mexican garrison. For the moment, the settlers had won; they were certain their titles would be honored by the local authorities, one of whom was Jim Bowie's father-in-law, Don Veramendi.

Soon the Royalist government in Mexico City was overthrown and the people of Texas felt their troubles were over. Shortly thereafter, on February 12, 1832, a son was born to Jim and Ursula Bowie.

In the past year Jim's business ventures had prospered. He had installed a steam mill for cotton spinning at the Veramendi summer home at Saltillo. The mill now operated night and day. Here Jim had used the same idea he had borrowed earlier in working out plans for the steam sugar mill back in Louisiana. He was happy now to spend his time with his wife and son; but soon this happiness was to end.

In August 1832 Jim learned that his brother was going blind. He left at once for Louisiana and then traveled with his brother to doctors in Cincinnati, New York, and Philadelphia. While Jim was away, an epidemic of cholera broke out in Texas, and Don Veramendi moved the entire family to Monclova thinking that the mountain air would be safe. In September cholera hit the area, and in three days' time the entire Veramendi family, Jim's wife and child, and several servants, died. Jim did not know of this tragedy until January.

Losing his family and many close friends was a terrible blow to Jim. He returned to his mother's home in Louisiana and thought he never wanted to see Texas again. But the spell of Texas was upon him, and in a few months he returned to San Antonio de Bexar, taking up residence in the old Veramendi Palace. While Jim was away, Texas had become bitterly divided between those who wanted an outright war with Mexico for independence and those who wanted to settle the problems of Texas peacefully. Jim Bowie agreed with those wanting peace.

Then in 1833 Santa Anna deposed the president and congress of Mexico and set himself up as dictator. It soon became clear that Santa Anna would not grant Texas independence without a war. Sam Houston had come to Texas, and he and Jim Bowie became friends. They had parallel ideas for working out the independence of Texas and neither man wanted an outright war with Santa Anna's forces at this time.

But Santa Anna soon sent an army, under General Martin Cos, to San Antonio de Bexar, and a battle was now inevitable. Jim Bowie was put in command of the volunteers and sent toward San Antonio. On their way to San Antonio, the volunteers met a force of Mexican soldiers at Mission La Purisima Concepcion. Due to Jim Bowie's able leadership, the Texans, though greatly outnumbered, won what history calls the Battle of Concepcion.

San Antonio was now occupied by General Cos's regular army, and the Texans lay siege to the town for more than a month. When reinforcements arrived, it was decided to storm the walls of the town. But Jim had a letter from Sam Houston, now commander-in-chief of the armies of Texas, asking him to report to San Felipe. He complied, leaving a few days before the battle for San Antonio began. After several days of close, hand-to-hand fighting, General Cos surrendered, and San Antonio de Bexar was again in the hands of the Texans.

Bowie and Houston were sure that the defeat of General Cos would bring Santa Anna and the Mexican army north to recover Texas, with San Antonio being the main target. Together, they asked the governor of Texas to let them recruit an army to meet Santa Anna when he crossed the Rio Grande. The governor thought this was a good

plan, but other members of the Texas Consultation Council disagreed.

Jim Bowie returned to San Antonio to command the volunteers. Later he was joined by Colonel Travis, in command of the regular army. These two men, who had disagreed before, now disagreed on the defense of San Antonio.

Colonel Travis did not think Santa Anna would march north at this time of the year. When he heard that the Mexican Army was on the march, he ordered his troops to leave San Antonio and take up the defense of the Mission San Antonio de Valero—the Alamo.

The old mission outside the walls of San Antonio was deserted, and much of it was in ruins, but its thick walls were still standing. Both Travis and Bowie believed it could be defended with their 150 men until help arrived. Sam Houston had ordered the Texas forces to destroy the Alamo and fall back to Gonzales and Copano. Bowie refused this order, knowing that Santa Anna must be defeated at the Alamo to save the settlements.

While helping to position a cannon on one of the walls of the Alamo, Bowie fell from the platform and was seriously injured. He was carried to the hospital, never again to leave his cot. Santa Anna's force of 5,000 soon occupied all of San Antonio and lay siege to the Alamo. At first the defenders were hopeful, since their scouts were able to carry requests for help across the Mexican lines. The siege lasted for 11 days. Then in the early morning of March 6, 1836, Santa Anna's forces stormed the walls of the Alamo. In the bloody, hand-to-hand combat that followed, their superior numbers soon overwhelmed the brave defenders.

Jim Bowie, propped up on his cot, was one of the last of the defenders to be killed. His last act was to bury his famous knife into the chest of one of the Mexicans who crossed the threshold. The defenders of the Alamo died heroically.

James Bridger
(Old Gabe)

1804-1881

VI

James Bridger
(Old Gabe)

1804–1881

Jim Bridger, hunter, trapper, fur trader, guide, and Mountain Man, was born on March 17, 1804, in Richmond, Virginia. He was one of three children. His father was a tavern keeper and part-time surveyor. When Jim was eight, the family headed West, and that journey over the Blue Ridge Mountains, the Blue Grass country, and through deep woods opened Jim's eyes to a new way of life.

The Bridgers reached the Mississippi and settled on a farm at a place called Six-Mile-Prairie not far from the frontier town of St. Louis. Jim was soon faced with a personal tragedy—the death of his mother, brother, and father. While still in his early teens, Jim was left with the task of providing for himself and his younger sister. Food was no problem. Jim raised vegetables and could shoot game. But clothes and other necessities had to be bought for cash. He needed a job. Jim's first job was ferrying teams and wagons across the Mississippi between Six-Mile-Prairie and St. Louis. This was a strenuous task for a youngster, but Jim was always available, day or night, and in all kinds of weather.

Jim then was offered the chance to become a blacksmith's apprentice. The five years Jim spent as an apprentice were profitable to him in many ways. He not only learned a trade, but also got to know the men who were opening up the West—men who were heroes to this young boy. St. Louis was the headquarters for companies that outfitted men, wagon trains, and boats for travel to the West.

At the end of Jim's apprenticeship, it seemed to him that everyone in St. Louis was getting ahead except him. St. Louis didn't need another blacksmith shop, and there was no job for him. He had no education and no capital to start a business. Then, three days after his 18th birthday, a brief notice in the local paper stated that "one hundred young men will be engaged to ascend the Missouri River to its source to trade with the Indians." Jim applied for the job and was hired as a trapper and Indian fighter. A new phase in his life had begun.

The expedition of the Rocky Mountain Fur Company was being led by Colonel William H. Ashley and Major Andrew Henry. The mode of travel was to be by keelboat, and two were being outfitted when Jim was hired. It was here that Jim met Mike Fink, King of the Keelboat Men, a famous character of the time, who was killed in a quarrel a few months later.

The company's plan was to travel upriver to the mountains, then to hunt and trap on the other side of the mountains for beaver fur, then much in demand. This was expected to be hard and dangerous work, as the country was peopled by hostile Indian tribes—Sioux, Blackfoot, Snakes, Assiniboines, and Rees.

JAME L. VLASATY

Almost from the first, the two boats had hard going. It rained almost every day and the river was full of debris. Then, about 20 miles below Fort Osage, one boat sank with more than $10,000 worth of supplies. Although every man was saved, this was a great loss and caused considerable hardship.

The company continued to have bad luck as the weeks passed. Indian raids cost them men's lives, equipment, and horses. At last they were forced to change their plans. Instead of going on to the Great Falls of the Missouri, they would have to stop at the mouth of the Yellowstone.

The plan of Ashley and Henry was for the trappers to set out on their own to trap, for which they would be paid a yearly salary for all fur taken. In this way the men could work year round without losing time traveling to St. Louis to sell their fur on the open market.

Jim began hunting and trapping, and it was soon clear that he had an unusual talent for it. He had the knack of finding the best places for beaver trapping and soon was familiar with the mountains, valleys, and rivers as no other. In other words, he was a born explorer — a true Mountain Man.

Jim, now 20, soon realized that he could not get ahead by working for Ashley and Henry. He had to become a "free trapper" and operate on his own. Breaking his ties with the Rocky Mountain Fur Company, Jim and several other men, set themselves up as a brigade of free trappers with Jim as their leader.

In the spring of 1824, Crow hunters told Jim and his men that many lodges of beaver were to be found beyond the South Pass. Exploring the area, Jim and Tom Fitzpatrick discovered Bridger Pass, the pass that opened the trail for hosts of emigrants over the Continental Divide and on into Oregon and California.

After the summer rendezvous where all free trappers went to sell their furs and to purchase supplies for the next season, Jim started out to find fresh trapping grounds. He traveled alone in a bullboat, a willow boat covered with buffalo skin. To win a bet with his men, he boated down the Bear River, exploring the country as he went along. Far away to the south, he found a great body of water. Reaching the shore, he tasted the water and found it salty.

Back in camp, Jim told of his discovery, and it was first thought that he had discovered an inlet of the Pacific Ocean. It was later determined that Jim Bridger had discovered the Great Salt Lake. He later explored the Fire Hole River and Yellowstone Lake.

In the years that followed, Jim and his men had many adventures as they traveled back and forth over the mountains from trapping grounds to the rendezvous to sell their fur.

In one skirmish with Indians, Jim was shot in the back with two arrows. One arrow-point was cut out, but he carried the other lodged deep in his back for years before

it, too, was removed. These Mountain Men were a tough, brave breed.

In some years the beaver harvest of Jim's brigade of free trappers came to thousands of dollars, but times were changing. The demand for beaver skins was falling off, as was the supply of beavers. The cost of getting their fur to the market in St. Louis was rising, as was the cost of getting supplies back. To make matters worse, the number of trapping companies competing against each other was growing. In some years there were hundreds of men trapping under Jim Bridger's authority, in other years only a few accompanied him.

In the spring of 1832, another famous frontiersman, Kit Carson, joined Bridger's party. He and Jim had many a fight with Indians, who were always stealing the horses and supplies of the trappers.

In 1835, when Jim was 31, he married the daughter of a Flathead Indian chief. Now he had not only a wife to provide for but many of her relatives as well, since this was an old Indian custom. From this union a daughter was born.

In 1835 Bridger took more than 500 trappers into winter quarters. It was a big camp and one of the last, for the demand for beaver fur was diminishing. For the next two years Jim and his men trapped in and around Yellowstone Park. The rendezvous in 1837 was a slim affair as the trappers had few beaver pelts to sell. The

next two years were worse, and early in 1839 Jim went to St. Louis—his first visit in years. He returned to spend two more years trapping beaver, but it began to look as if his days in the mountains were at an end. In earlier years he had owned hundreds of horses and had been a leader of men and a great chief to the Indians. He now found himself poor, lonesome, and, since trapping had come to an end, without work. What could he do to support himself and his family?

In 1841 Jim and several friends headed toward Fort Laramie, the principal trading post on the Oregon Trail. There he once again met Kit Carson, who was then acting as a guide. While at the Fort, several emigrant trains on their way to Oregon and California stopped to buy supplies and horses and to repair their wagons. Jim immediately saw his opportunity. He would build a trading post deeper in the mountains. With his early training as a blacksmith and his knowledge of the mountains, he was sure his trading post would become an important stopping place for settlers crossing the mountains.

After several months of planning, Jim started building on Black's Fork of Green River in Wyoming, and with an old friend, Louis Vasquez, as a partner, founded Fort Bridger in 1843. It was a successful business venture from the start. No one knew the mountains, the Indians, and the hardships of life better than Jim Bridger. To spare his daughter the hardship of life at the fort, Jim sent her to a mission school for an education.

Jim still left from time to time to trap and hunt, but he was usually kept busy at the fort. Many parties came by in 1846. Among them was the ill-fated Donner party, which later lost so many when they were trapped by snow on the Sierra Nevadas. The next summer the Mormons, led by Brigham Young, passed through, looking for a place to settle. Jim Bridger and Brigham Young had many conferences, and Jim told him of the wonders of the Great Basin, or Salt Lake valley, which Jim had discovered years before and had always considered "his paradise." Young and the Mormons finally settled in the valley.

The winter of 1847 kept Jim at the fort, and one day he was visited by an old trapper friend, Joe Meek. Meek brought bad news. The Indians had attacked the mission school, murdering everyone but Jim's daughter, who was carried off alive. This was a severe blow to Jim, who knew he would never see his daughter again. Still another tragedy occurred when Jim's wife died during the birth of their second daughter. He later married a woman from the Snake Tribe who bore him several children.

From time to time Jim acted as a guide for the Army. He was able to find new routes for all travelers, and one of them was later used by the Overland Stage, the Pony Express, and the Union Pacific Railroad.

In 1851 the government called the Sioux, Cheyennes, Arapahos, Crows, Assiniboines, Mandans, Snakes, and Rees into council at Laramie to sign a treaty. Jim Bridger, the only man who had the respect of most of the tribes and could understand their language and their customs, acted as interpreter. After days of talking, feasting, and arguing, the treaty was signed, only to be broken many times in the years ahead.

When the Mormons first settled around Great Salt Lake, they were friendly, as they needed supplies and all the help they could get from Fort Bridger. Later they became hostile, and Brigham Young made up his mind to drive Jim Bridger and all other Mountain Men from the region. In 1853 the Mormons raided Fort Bridger,

driving Jim into the mountains. They destroyed the fort, with all its merchandise, livestock, and buildings. All his possessions were lost; this was the end of Fort Bridger. Once again, Jim found himself out of work.

But "Old Gabe," as Jim was now known, knew the mountains, trails, and the Indians possibly better than most men of his time, so he was always in demand as guide. For several years he guided the party of Sir George Gore, a sportsman from Ireland. He made many trips in the area of Yellowstone Park and later to Fort Union, then the largest trading post in the West, owned by the American Fur Company.

The Mormon War of 1857 caught up with Jim, and he was hired by the Army as a scout. The Mormons were soon brought under control, ending for all time their efforts to set up an independent state. Jim then joined his family at a small farm at Little Santa Fe.

In the years to come, Jim Bridger was guide and scout for several Army expeditions to mark out routes for future settlers. But "Old Gabe" was getting old and could not stand the hardship of travel as he did in his younger days.

In January 1865 he was called into service as chief of scouts for the Powder River expedition under General Grenville Dodge. The government was still trying to sign a treaty with the Indians, but did not succeed with the Sioux, the most troublesome of all the tribes, until 1868. Jim was later called back into service with General Phil Sheridan, but this job lasted only a few months.

Jim now retired to a small place in Missouri, a few miles from Kansas City. He was in ill health and his sight began to fail. At last, totally blind, he could only walk around the house and grounds, often with the neighborhood children, who always liked to hear him tell of his adventures.

The end came on July 17, 1881, and Jim Bridger, whose name is still remembered at Bridger Peak, Bridger Pass, Bridger Mountain, Bridger Lake, Bridger Road, and many other places in the West, went to his reward.

Christopher (Kit) Carson

1809-1868

VII
Christopher (Kit) Carson
1809–1868

Lindsay and Rebecca Carson had journeyed from the East late in the eighteenth century to make their new home in the wilderness area of Kentucky near present-day Richmond. It was here, on December 24, 1809, that the last of their five sons, Kit Carson, was born.

By the time of Kit's birth, this part of the country had been tamed. There were no animals to trap or Indians to fight. The hard life of the early frontier was over. There were still no schools, but Kit's mother taught him what little she knew. Kit differed from many frontiersmen in that he could read and write.

But, like other boys of his time, Kit longed for the adventurous life of the frontiers. With four older brothers as examples, he soon learned to ride, and shoot. He became an expert with pistols and rifles at an early age.

When Kit was five, his father rebelled at the restrictions of civilization in Kentucky. He sold his farm and moved the family to Howard County, Missouri, then deep in the wilderness.

This was the life for Kit. He stalked deer, shot buffalo, and brought in wild ducks for the table. He became acquainted with the Osage Indians and soon could speak their dialect. But, since not all the Indians were friendly, the Carsons had to move into a fort for safety. Anyone leaving the fort to farm or hunt had to be accompanied by riflemen. Needless to say, these restrictions were not to Kit's liking. He wanted to be out and away from the confines of the fort, learning the ways of the wilderness.

By the time Kit Carson was 12, he was expected to do his share of work—as well as his lessons. He was small for his age, and, to overcome what he thought was a handicap, he always volunteered for the hardest work. As a result, he grew into a strong and healthy man. Whenever he was free of chores or studies, he rode his horse, a gift from his father.

Kit at 15 was ready to move west — something his father could understand well enough. But his mother was reluctant to let him go, although it was plain that he wasn't a farmer, like his father and brothers. At last his parents decided to apprentice him to a saddler, and Kit spent two years learning about leather. This was to be a help to him in the years following, but he never gave up his desire to explore the unknown territory of the West.

In the spring of 1826, a small party of traders on their way to Santa Fe stopped in Kit's village to buy supplies. Kit, now 17, applied for a place in the party, and, after demonstrating his skill with both pistol and rifle, he was accepted. Kit said goodbye to his parents and brothers, and the part of his life that was to make him a folk hero began.

But the beginning was not easy. Only the leader of the party had ever been west of the Missouri; the rest were inexperienced men. Although Kit was the youngest, he knew more than all the others about how to live off the land. The party was always short of food and in trouble with the Indians. But at last they reached Santa Fe, sold their merchandise, and disbanded.

Kit liked what he saw in Mexico — the people, the country, and the climate were strange and exciting. He decided to stay on and become a fur trader. He spent the winter near Santa Fe with a trader by the name of Kincaid, who taught him Spanish and several Indian dialects he would need as a trader.

But things were not to come easy for Kit. He could not find a job as a trapper, because he had had no experience. He started for home, met another party headed for Santa Fe, and returned with them as a guard. Kit next went to Taos, where he worked as a cook and as a teamster at the copper mines nearby.

In 1829 Kit at last had his chance to become a trapper. He joined a party of men, and together they trapped beaver and fought Indians all the way to California and back. Beaver skins were bringing high prices, and Kit did well when the party disbanded back in Taos in April, 1830. Now an experienced trapper, Kit went to the unsettled Utah and Oregon territories with the party of Thomas Fitzpatrick, a famous Mountain Man.

By 1832 Kit Carson, now 23, had not only money of his own, but a reputation as a man who could be relied on, a good trapper, an excellent shot, and a leader of men. The image of Kit Carson had been formed.

For the next few years Kit moved from place to place and from company to company, trapping, fighting Indians, and selling his furs at the yearly rendezvous. Fur

and food were sometimes plentiful, sometimes scarce. But there was always trouble with the Indians.

Kit was always careful with his money, and though his savings were once wiped out by a bank failure, he was destined to become a wealthy man.

By 1839 Kit was ready for something new. He didn't want to spend his whole life as a Mountain Man. More and more settlers were moving west, and Kit decided to go to work for one of the trading companies that served them. Since Bent and St. Vrain was the largest and most prosperous of these companies, Kit went to work for them as a professional hunter at their post in Colorado County, Bent's Fort.

While working at Bent's Fort, Kit met a party of Cheyenne Indians, and, since he was known to their chief, they invited him to their village. There Kit and the daughter of the chief fell in love and were married. She was named Rai-Du, meaning Mountain Flower, but Kit called her Alice. The winter of 1839-40 Kit and his wife spent at Bent's Fort. Late in 1840 Mrs. Carson died while giving birth to a daughter. Now Kit faced the problem of finding a home for his infant daughter, Mary.

In 1842 Kit returned to his boyhood home to find both parents long dead, his brothers gone, the family house in ruins, and the farm abandoned. He was a stranger to most of the neighbors, but from one he learned that his brother Robert lived in St. Louis. Kit went to St. Louis and a happy reunion with his brother, who agreed to give Mary a home and to see to her education. After a few days Kit started back to Bent's Fort by steamboat. On board he met John C. Fremont, who had been given the difficult task of charting a route to the mouth of the Columbia River on the Pacific. He and Kit became friends, and soon Kit was hired as a guide for the Fremont Expedition. This chance meeting was to prove valuable to both, and Kit was to receive honors along with Fremont in the years to come. The Fremont party started out late in 1842 through the towering Wind River mountains and mapped a route to Fort Laramie.

Kit next went to Taos to represent the firm of St. Vrain. There he met and married a Mexican woman, Maria Jaramillo. They bought a house in Taos, and Kit immediately wrote his brother in St. Louis to request that his daughter be sent out to them. Later Maria bore three children, and Kit's first daughter, Mary, was a devoted older sister to them.

Kit was soon asked to act again as a guide for Fremont, who was to map a route to Oregon and Washington. Kit joined Fremont's party west of Bent's Fort. After many fights with Indians and suffering from exposure and lack of food, the party finally cut through the Blue Mountains to the Columbia River and on to the Pacific. The party continued south, nearly becoming lost in the deep snows of the Sierra Nevadas. But after weeks of struggle, and due to Kit's knowledge of the country, the explorers staggered into Sutter's Fort on March 6, 1844. The march had been the longest in the history of such expeditions, as they had left Kansas on May 29, 1843. After a month's rest, the expedition headed back to Bent's Fort.

Kit now decided to give up the hard life of a Mountain Man to settle down with his family. In the spring of 1845, he bought land near Taos, built a house, and began to farm. But a summons from his friend Fremont soon put an end to farming. Kit sold his farm at a great loss and again joined Fremont in exploring and mapping new territory and routes. Today Carson's explorations are remembered in such places as Carson Lake, Carson River, and the huge salt deposit, Carson Sink, as well as Carson City, Nevada.

The Fremont party worked its way west and south, again coming to Sutter's Fort in California. There, since the Mexican War was being fought, the party was enrolled as militiamen under Fremont, who held the rank of an army captain. Fremont marched to Monterey, and, with the help of a squadron of navy ships, captured Los Angeles and San Diego. Fremont then sent Kit in the direction of New Mexico with dispatches for the War department. On the way he met a regiment under Colonel S. W. Kearny, who kept Kit as a guide and sent the dispatches on by others. Kit was soon battling the Mexicans, but before long the hold of Mexico on the California territory was broken forever.

In March 1847 Kearny sent Kit and several other enlisted men to Washington with dispatches. They arrived in June. This was Kit Carson's first visit to the nation's capital, and he was overcome by all the attention paid him. He had become a celebrity due to the accounts sent in by Fremont and Kearny. Even though Washington was still in some ways a primitive place, Kit Carson created a sensation in his stained buckskins and worn moccasins with his long rifle slung over his shoulder.

While in Washington, Kit was called in by President James K. Polk, who questioned him about the current state of affairs in California. After their conversation the President offered Kit a commission as a first lieutenant in the Army. He was later sworn in at the War Department and turned in his buckskins for a new army uniform. Soon he received orders to carry dispatches across the continent to Kearny, who had been promoted to brigadier general. The journey took Kit to Bent's Fort. There, to his surprise, he was reunited with his wife and daughters, who had been forced to leave Taos during the war and who had journeyed to the fort for safety. After a short stay, Kit resumed his journey to General Kearny in Monterey.

Kit passed the winter of 1847-48 with the soldiers under General Kearny. Soon word was received that General Scott had captured Mexico City; the war with Mexico was over. In March 1848 Kit again was ordered to carry dispatches to Washington and reached Taos in time to meet his family returning from Bent's Fort. After a few weeks in Taos and Santa Fe, he went on to Washington, where he received his army pay and the wages due him for Fremont's third expedition. Kit, now wealthier by several thousand dollars, returned to Taos to renew kinship with the family he scarcely knew. He was now 39 and looked forward to a quiet and uneventful life with his wife and children. But the adventures of Kit Carson were far from over.

The southwest, now under American administrators, was changing and fast becoming settled. Kit Carson, with money to invest, began to plan his future. He bought a large tract of land, and soon ranch houses, barns, and other buildings began to take shape. In the summer of 1849, Kit and his family moved into their new home. The ranch prospered, and Kit's future was assured. Life was not always pleasant—the Apache Indians continued to raid and steal. Kit and other former Mountain Men often helped in battling the Indians. In May 1850 Kit and a neighbor drove a band of horses and mules more than 500 miles to Fort Laramie and sold them at sky-high prices to emigrants on their way to the California gold fields. In 1851 Kit took a wagon train laden with wheat, oats, and rye to St. Louis.

Returning to the ranch for the winter, he soon became restless again. The ranch was being well-managed by his foreman and the quiet life of a farmer was never quite enough for Kit. In 1853 he drove 6500 head of sheep to California and sold them at a profit of $25,000. While in California, he visited his brother Moses and revisited San Francisco, now much different from the colorless mud village he had seen years earlier. Kit returned to Taos by a new trail through what are now Arizona and New Mexico. On returning home in December 1853, he found a letter informing him that President Franklin Pierce had appointed him Indian agent for the territory.

Nowhere was the post of Indian agent more important than the New Mexico Territory, and nowhere was there a person more experienced for the job than Kit Carson. The Indians had been pushed farther and farther west and were now being slowly hemmed in by civilization. In this territory, which included the future states of New Mexico, Arizona, and Colorado, lived the Comanche,

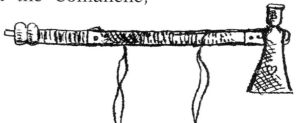

Cheyenne, Navajo, Arapaho, and Apache Indians. Kit not only knew the Indians and their way of life, but was known to their chiefs as well.

Kit's ranch was in the so-called Rayado, near Taos, and it was here that he established his post. Soon afterward he was able to put down a small Apache uprising because he knew the chief of the warriors, and they trusted him and the promises he made on behalf of the government. But, as with so many promises made by the government to the Indians, they were not kept. The Apaches and their allies, the Utah Indians from the mountains to the north, soon were raiding, stealing, and killing again. The government was forced to send in soldiers, and Kit was called into service as a guide. Many engagements were fought during the years 1854-55 but never a decisive battle. Kit spent most of this time with the soldiers. His family rarely saw him, but that was how it had always been. The Apache War of 1856 finally brought the Indians under control, and Kit was able to spend the next few years at the ranch at Rayado.

Kit Carson was by now a national figure both in and out of government. News accounts, magazine articles, books, all pictured him in glowing terms—to his embarrassment and dismay, because most of these accounts were highly exaggerated.

The chiefs of the many tribes visited his ranch and were always made welcome. Kit sympathized with their grievances and helped them in any way that he could.

In April 1861 the Civil War began, and the only prolonged period of peace Kit Carson had ever known was about to be broken. The New Mexico Territory stood as a buffer between Confederate Texas and Unionist California. Slavery did not exist here, and the people had not been concerned with the problems of the states. Now, however, a decision had to be made. Many favored the Confederate cause, but Kit Carson remained loyal to the Union and was one of the first New Mexicans to offer his services. He was granted a territorial commission as lieutenant colonel of the First New Mexican Volunteer

Infantry in May, 1861, and soon found himself engaged in combat with Confederate forces. On September 20, 1861, he was promoted to the rank of full colonel.

The two armies spent the better part of 1861-62 in minor battles, since the troops on both sides were untrained. Then, on February 21, 1862, the Battle of Valverde was fought, breaking the Confederate hold on the territory. It was followed on March 28-29 by the Battle of Apache Canyon. The Confederate Army, defeated, withdrew from New Mexico.

During the Civil War the Indians again took to the war path. Now it was the powerful Navajos who were raiding and killing. The Navajos were a nation of 10,000, and Kit Carson commanded an army of 700. Nevertheless, Kit was ordered to wage a campaign. This was undoubtedly his most brilliant undertaking. Rather than meet the Navajos in battle, Kit destroyed their villages, livestock, and fields, and the Indians finally surrendered in April 1864. Kit had not enjoyed waging this campaign. He was in sympathy with the Indians and felt that they were being treated unfairly by the government. But he had done his duty and completed his mission successfully.

Other tribes were now on the war path. Treaties were torn up, and again Kit was sent against the warriors. On November 25, 1864, Kit fought and was beaten by the

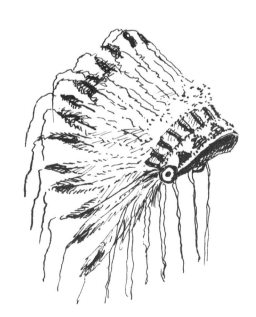

Comanche and Kiowa at the Battle of Adobe Walls. Kit's forces were forced to retire, but the Indians, too, suffered heavy casualties.

For the next three years, Kit continued to try to subdue and control the Indians. In 1865 Colonel Christopher Carson was promoted to the rank of brigadier general. He was responsible for a vast domain: New Mexico, Colorado, Utah, Idaho, Dakota, and Arizona. He remained in the field constantly. In October 1867 he was thrown from his horse and severely injured. He returned to his home, and due to this injury, was retired from the army.

In January 1868 he was appointed Indian agent for southeastern Colorado by President Andrew Johnson. He and his wife moved to Boggsville, later renamed La Junta. On April 23, Mrs. Carson died, and this loss so affected Kit that his health declined rapidly. On May 26 he suffered a heart attack. Early on the morning of May 28 Kit Carson, Mountain Man and brigadier general of the Army, died peacefully in his own bed at the age of 58.

James Butler Hickok
(Wild Bill)

1837-1876

VIII
James Butler Hickok
(Wild Bill)

1837–1876

His name was James Butler Hickok, but he was known as "Wild Bill," and the nickname was rightfully earned. Born in Troy Grove, LaSalle County, Illinois, on May 27, 1837, James was named after his mother's father. His parents were William Alonzo and Polly Butler Hickok. Jim was the last of four boys; later two other children, both girls, were born.

He was raised in a small log house in a remote village. Even as a small boy, Jim was fond of guns and, whenever he could, he slipped into the woods to practice with an old pistol he had been given. Jim was a loner, preferring his own company to that of his brothers and sisters. He carried this quality into adulthood — and was sometimes disliked for it. An independent boy became an independent man. Fortunately his father insisted that he have some schooling, although his education was very limited.

William Alonzo Hickok's business ventures failed in the financial panic of 1837 and he turned to farming to support his family. Later he built a tavern, called the Green Mountain House, which served as an "underground railroad" station where escaped slaves were concealed until they could be taken north to freedom. Jim heard his first shot fired in anger when officers found two escaped slaves hidden in their northbound wagon.

Jim's father died in 1852, leaving the running of the farm in his sons' hands. Jim, being the youngest, was to supply food. This was a task he enjoyed, since supplying deer and small game for the table gave him all the shooting he wanted. This made him a crack shot at 17.

Jim also took on several temporary jobs driving wagons and as a towpath driver on the newly opened Illinois and Michigan Canal. Late in 1855 Jim left home for the West not to return for 14 years.

Jim settled in the small village of Mill Creek, in Johnson County, Kansas, where he worked for a time as a plowman. Trouble was brewing on the Kansas-Missouri border—deep trouble that promoted the Civil War—so Hickok served in the Free-State Army of Kansas for over a year, until things were somewhat settled. Hickok was with the ill-fated Lew Simpson wagon train when it was attacked and destroyed by Mormons on October 5, 1857. Hickok managed to save 11-year old Will Cody (Buffalo Bill) from a beating by camp ruffians and they were friends for life.

In 1858 Hickok went to work for the firm of Russell, Majors, and Waddell, the company that started the Pony Express. Hickok did not serve as a Pony Express rider, being too tall and over 21, but for nearly two years he drove wagons and stagecoaches from Santa Fe to Fort Lyon, Colorado, and on other routes owned by the company. It was during this time that he met Jack Slade, the line superintendent of the stagecoach division. One night Indians drove off the horses from one of the Pony Express stops, leaving some 40 drivers and stocktenders idle. The men elected Hickok captain, and he, Slade, and some of the others rode after the Indians, recapturing the horses and about a hundred Indian ponies. Slade, during his lifetime, had reputedly killed 26 men; in later years Hickok was called "the Slade of Kansas," a title that annoyed him and certainly was unjustified.

The afternoon of Friday July 12, 1861, was an unforgettable day in the life of James Butler Hickok. On this day three men met their death, and fame came to one other. The tragedy took place about six miles from Fairbury, Nebraska, at East Rock Creek, a Pony Express station being run by Hickok. The station had been purchased by the Russell, Majors, and Waddell firm from one David McCanles but only a part of the purchase price had been paid. Hickok got into an argument with McCanles and two men with him over the balance of the money. Words led to gunplay, and Hickok killed all three opponents.

Hickok was acquitted in the trial that followed, but the legend of Wild Bill Hickok had begun.

After the McCanles affair, Hickok left Rock Creek and journeyed to Fort Leavenworth where he enlisted in the Union Army as a scout. During the Civil War Hickok served as a scout and courier, but his most important role was as a spy. In March 1862 he was detailed to report the movements of Confederate forces in Missouri and Arkansas, and he distinguished himself by bringing valued information through enemy lines to General Samuel R. Curtis. In the years 1862-64, Civil War legends grew around Wild Bill Hickok.

After the surrender of the Confederate forces in 1865, Hickok went to Springfield, Missouri, and to another Friday adventure. It was July 21, 1865. Springfield was a frontier town inhabited by strange and half-civilized people. The trouble started over a card game with Dave Tutt. Tutt lost and accused Hickok of owing him money, arguing until Hickok left the table. The next day Hickok and Tutt met walking across the public square, and both men pulled their pistols. Tutt was killed. Hickok was again arrested and again acquitted, but this time public opinion was against him. He was happy to leave Springfield and answer the summons of the government to serve as a U.S. deputy marshall.

Hickok journeyed to Fort Riley, Kansas, in February 1866 to accept his new assignment. He found Fort Riley a big, brawling, lawless town where decent folks were intimidated by soldiers, scouts, and emigrants who used the fort as a jumping off place. Wild Bill's orders were clear: "Clean up the town." This he did, not by force of arms or by killing, but by sheer strength of character. Before long a semblance of order was attained, and Wild Bill settled down to his normal duties. During this time Hickok met Lieutenant Colonel George Armstrong Custer, who was forming the new Seventh Cavalry Regiment.

Official duties as a deputy marshall occupied much of Hickok's time during 1867-69. But, with his friend Buffalo Bill, he also served as a scout. For nearly two years, he worked under General Winfield Hancock, who had been ordered to force the Cheyennes and Kiowas back to their reservations. Hickok also served briefly under Custer and the ill-fated Seventh Cavalry. Wounded in the leg by a Cheyenne warrior, Hickok retired as a scout in February, 1869. Soon he left for Troy Grove, having learned that his seriously ill mother wanted to see him. James Butler Hickok, the now famous "Wild Bill," had been absent from home for more than 14 years. Arriving in April, it was a joyous reunion for all, as a brother and his two sisters were also there. Jim, the youngest son, whose famous name was now second to none on the frontier, had come home! Jim's recent wound was becoming increasingly painful, and he agreed to an operation. He was satisfied for a time to rest and recover at home. But it soon grew dull and "Wild Bill" became restless to return to the wild and hard life of the frontier towns. But without a job and with dwindling funds, he seemed trapped. Then a letter arrived from a Senator Henry Wilson requesting his services.

The senator wanted Wild Bill to act as a guide for a party of men and women anxious to see the frontier towns and territory of the West. This was the opportunity Hickok was waiting for. He accepted and met the senator's party at Hays City, Kansas. When the party left on June 12, 1869, many people in Hays City predicted that the party of "fool dudes" would never return. But Wild Bill had planned the trip with care, and everyone returned safely after several weeks, with pleasant memories and generous praise for Hickok. Senator Wilson later gave a dinner for Hickok in New York and presented him with a beautiful pair of Colt revolvers that he cherished all his life.

Once again Wild Bill was jobless, but with an established law enforcement reputation. On August 23, 1869, he was elected sheriff of Ellis County, Kansas, with headquarters at Hays. Hays was a rapidly growing town, a meeting place for buffalo hunters, skinners, trappers, and gamblers, and the terminus of the Union Pacific Railroad. It was also a "wild" town—saloon keeping was the most profitable business—and the permanent residents were alarmed at the increasing violence. Hickok posted anti-firearm notices, but found enforcement difficult in the lawless town of Hays. Three days after he took office, Hickok was forced to gun down a man by the name of Mulrey.

Wild Bill was an officer who would uphold the law—but he was also a gambler. In a dispute over a game of cards, Hickok killed a man by the name of Strawhim, well-known in Hays as a ruffian and gambler. Hickok was tried for this killing and acquitted on testimony that he was acting in the line of duty. Some did not agree with this decision, and Hickok's brief term as a peace officer in Hays was ended in December 1869. He then went to Ellsworth for a few weeks and then on to Topeka.

In July 1870 Hickok, still without a permanent job, returned to Hays. There he was involved in a fight with some soldiers from nearby Fort Hays. Hickok killed one and seriously wounded another. To avoid being jailed and possibly hanged by the army, Hickok left town in a hurry. Hickok next joined the Ginger Circus at Sherman, Texas, but left at the end of one performance.

The remainder of the winter 1870-71 passed uneventfully for Wild Bill Hickok. Bored with gambling, in February he took a train to Fort Hooker, hoping to sign up as an army scout. There he met an old friend who offered him the job of marshall of Abilene, Kansas. His salary was to be $150 a month and 25 percent of all fines.

Abilene was the first of the famous cowtowns of Kansas. A rough, tough, new town, it was the Texas cowboy who made Abilene the place it was. After months of hard work on the trail during the cattle drive, he was ready for all that Abilene had to offer. Wild Bill knew he had a real job ahead of him. He had not only the cowhands to deal with but the crooked saloonkeepers and gamblers who employed any means, fair or foul, to take the cowhands' pay. One of Hickok's three deputies was Tom Carson, nephew of Kit Carson.

Wild Bill tried to keep the peace, but peace was not what the cowboys wanted in Abilene. Hickok, disliked by both the Texans and the saloonkeepers, was always fearful of assassination. He had reason to worry, since he had only himself and three deputies to handle as many as 5,000 Texas cowboys. For the first few months, Hickok was able to control this unruly mob without bloodshed, but a killing was inevitable.

In October, 1871, it happened. Hickok was trying to move a drunken mob of cowboys off the main street of Abilene when their leader, Phil Cole, pulled a gun. Hickok, being the faster, fired both his revolvers first. One bullet killed Cole outright. The other accidentally hit and killed a policeman.

This double tragedy sounded the death knell for Abilene. Two months later, the citizens and farmers persuaded the city fathers to ban the cattle trade.

The end of the cattle trade also meant the end of Hickok's job as marshall. But Abilene had done something for James Butler Hickok: it had spread his legend down the trail to Texas and added considerably to it. If his fame was not assured earlier, it certainly was after his service at Abilene.

Wild Bill moved on, first to Georgetown, Colorado, then to Kansas City, where he took over as house gambler in one of the large saloons. Then he was invited to appear in a Wild West Show and Buffalo Hunt at Niagara Falls, Canada, in August 1872.

Then, Hickok joined his friend Buffalo Bill Cody in the stage play *The Scouts of the Plains*. The show was a success—even with untrained actors, who often forgot their lines. But in spite of the play's success, Hickok was unhappy. It meant being sociable with people from the audience and with others in the troupe. It meant being on time for performances and traveling by a timetable. None of these things suited Hickok — especially since Cody seemed to be getting all the main parts. When the show played at Rochester, New York, on March 10, 1874, Hickok received an urgent message from General Phil Sheridan urging him to join the troops at Fort Laramie for an important scouting mission. This was what Wild Bill had been looking for: an excuse to leave. Although Cody tried to keep him, Hickok left the show never to return.

There is no official record that Hickok ever served with General Sheridan after leaving the Buffalo Bill Show. From Rochester he went to New York, where he gambled away his savings. Finding it difficult to settle in one place, he drifted to Kansas City, Denver, and, at last, Cheyenne, Wyoming.

In its early days, Cheyenne was an end-of-the-track railroad boom town second only to Abilene as the toughest, roughest, and wildest place on the continent. By 1874 Cheyenne was beginning to settle down as more and more permanent residents made it their home. Soon after Wild Bill arrived, an old friend arrived—Madame Lake of the Lake Circus. On March 5, 1876, Mrs. Agnes Lake Thatcher and James Butler Hickok were married. The couple left that night by train for the bride's home in Cincinnati. Two weeks later Hickok, at 39, with failing eyesight, jobless, and without means of supporting a wife, set off to make his fortune in the gold-rich Black Hills of South Dakota. He left his wife, promising to send for her as soon as he made a "strike." She never saw him again.

Wild Bill first joined a group of miners at St. Louis, then went to Cheyenne, where he joined an old friend,

Colorado Charlie Utter. From Cheyenne they and several others headed for Deadwood, the headquarters for all types of humanity hoping to strike it rich: miners, gamblers, saloonkeepers, con men, and many of the famous frontiersmen of the time. Hickok's party made camp on Whitewood Creek close to Deadwood and soon staked out several nearby claims they hoped would produce.

Once it was known in Deadwood that Wild Bill was in town, old friends began to look him up. Turning to cards to pay expenses, Hickok gambled at every opportunity. Many former enemies, as well as saloonkeepers and gamblers, resented him, thinking he was in Deadwood to impose law and order as he had in Abilene. The end came on August 2, 1876, only 20 days after his arrival in Deadwood.

The day was hot, and, after working through the morning at the claim, Hickok changed to his favorite outfit— a Prince Albert with all the trimmings. Late in the afternoon he went to the Number Ten Saloon to gamble. Wild Bill consistently played with his back to the wall so that no one could get behind him. On this occasion, however, another player had that chair, and Hickok sat with his back to an open door. The tragedy happened so fast even the three players at the table were not aware Hickok had been shot until it was over.

About five minutes after Wild Bill started playing, Jack McCall, a small, furtive man, staggered in, drew his revolver and shot Hickok in the back of his head. Wild Bill was killed instantly, the bullet entering the base of the brain, exiting through the right cheek, and imbedding itself in the left wrist of a Captain Massie, one of the other players at the table. The time was 4:10 P.M.

So ended the short, tragic career of James Butler "Wild Bill" Hickok: scout, spy, pistoleer, gambler, peace officer, miner, and showman. Possibly not always the superhero that folklore has made him, Wild Bill was nonetheless one of the most colorful of our famous frontiersmen.

George Armstrong Custer

1839-1876

IX
George Armstrong Custer
1839–1876

It was on a Sunday afternoon in June, 1876, that one of the most colorful men of the early West met his death. The mystery of the death of George Armstrong Custer and the 225 soldiers with him will probably never be solved; there were no survivors.

George Armstrong Custer was born on a small farm near New Rumley, at that time in Harrison County, Ohio, on December 5, 1839. His father was Emmanuel Custer, a widower with three children, who had married a widow with three children. George was the first of three children born to this union. The Custers came of fighting stock, as the great-grandfather of young Custer had been a Hessian mercenary in the Revolutionary War.

It seemed that a war of one kind or another was always in the background as Custer grew into manhood. He was seven years old when the Mexican War began and his father joined the local militia. Although many boys his age liked hunting, Custer's interest in guns was not as a hunter but as a soldier. He dreamed of marching off with Generals Scott and Taylor in the Mexican campaign. But his family had other plans for him.

At the age of ten, Custer was sent to Monroe, Michigan, where he lived with a step-sister and attended Stebbins Academy. He spent four of the next six years at the academy. When he returned to the Custer farm at 16, he had already made up his mind to become an officer and professional soldier. He asked his father for help in getting an appointment to West Point, but his father, a Democrat, refused to write to the Republican congressman from their district, Congressman Bingham. Not to be put off, Custer himself wrote Congressman Bingham, but the appointment went to another applicant. The next year Custer met personally with Congressman Bingham, who was so impressed with Custer and his intense desire to enter West Point that he arranged the appointment. In 1858 George Armstrong Custer stepped off the Hudson River-Albany boat and walked up the steep incline to the academy grounds of West Point.

Custer's years at West Point were not to his credit. It was not that he was uninterested or stupid—he simply did not take studying and winning cadet honors seriously. As a result he was always rated among the lowest in his class. At the end of his third year, he came into his own at the bottom—Number 57 in a class of 57; and upon graduation, Number 35 in a class of 35. His record at the Point lists several hundred offenses against Cadet Custer, and West Point may never have had an officer more unsuited to tiresome discipline.

Abraham Lincoln was elected President on November 6, 1860, and the southern states soon began seceding from the Union. West Point cadets from southern states began to leave the Academy to enter the Confederate Army. The regular class of 1861 was pushed forward and graduated in May, but it was not until July 17, 1861, that Cadet George A. Custer was relieved from duty at West Point and ordered to report to the Adjutant General in Washington, D.C. He was assigned as a lieutenant to the Second Cavalry.

Custer did not have long to wait for the action he had craved since boyhood. Three days after leaving West Point, he found himself in the fury of battle at Bull Run, a crushing defeat for the Union forces. He was then transferred and appointed aide to Brigadier General Phil

had been drilled into what Custer expected of soldiers who served under him.

But General Sheridan had forced Smith to surrender, and the Mexican War did not come; late in the spring of 1865, Custer's division was disbanded. Custer was reduced from a major general of volunteers to a lowly captain in the regular army. He returned to Monroe, Michigan, where he was urged to run for public office. He declined, saying, "My life was destined and will be that of a soldier." After a short rest in Monroe, Custer went to Washington to see if he could get a leave of absence from the Army to accept an offer to become inspector general of cavalry in the Mexican Army at an enormous salary. Custer talked it over with General Grant, who wrote a letter in his behalf to the Secretary of War; but the Secretary refused to grant Custer leave.

Custer, disgusted, decided to appeal directly to President Johnson. But, instead of granting Custer leave to go to Mexico, Johnson ordered him and his wife to join the President's party on his "swing around the circuit." This was an honor—but not what Custer wanted.

For a period of thirty years, from 1830 to the beginning of the Civil War, there had been little trouble with the Plains Indians. Then in the 1840's the covered wagons headed for California and Oregon began to cross the plains that were the hunting grounds of the Indians. More and more followed in the 1850's. Then, with the discovery of gold, thousands poured across Indian lands, fighting the red man, trading bad whiskey for their furs and ponies, and spreading hate and fear. As the Indians began to rebel, the government built forts to protect the settlers and the gold seekers, ignoring the treaty rights of the Indians. Finally the army was sent to force the Indians onto reservations.

On July 28, 1866, Custer received his commission as lieutenant colonel of the newly authorized Seventh Cavalry and was ordered to report to Fort Riley, Kansas. This turned out to be another trying task for Custer, since the men of the regiment had enlisted only to be sent out

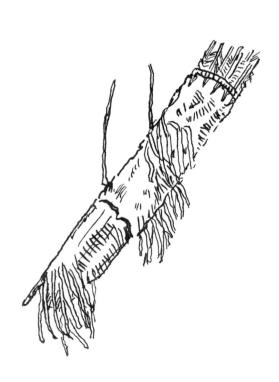

West, where they could desert and join the gold seekers. After months of hard work and discipline, however, Custer had the regiment in shape. Many engagements with the Indians were fought during the year, but not all of them were won by the army. The Indians were now well-mounted and equipped with the latest rifles and plenty of ammunition, supplied by unscrupulous Indian traders. It was during this period that Custer was court-martialed for an unauthorized move from one area to another and for taking leave to visit his wife. The charges were brought by officers jealous of his superior rank. Custer was convicted and sentenced to suspension of rank and pay for one year, but was recalled to service after eight months by his old Civil War commander, General Phil Sheridan.

Custer again took over the Seventh Cavalry and at once became involved in various Indian campaigns. Custer was always victorious, yet he sympathized with the Indians' viewpoint and thought the government was handling Indian affairs badly. These views may have given his officers new grounds for resenting Custer.

Custer's Indian victories added greatly to his reputation; once a great Civil War general, he was now considered one of the army's most successful Indian fighters.

In July 1867 General Sherman met with the chiefs of the Sioux nation, and the treaty of 1868 was agreed upon. The forts along the Bozeman Trail were to be dismantled and a tract of land set aside for the Sioux nation. For three years there was no serious trouble with the Indians. Then the Northern Pacific Railroad started laying track across the finest buffalo lands of the Sioux, and the Indians could see that the government did not intend to keep the terms of the treaty. The chiefs reasoned that their hunting grounds would soon be gone. The Indians would be forced onto reservations, there to be cheated by Indian agents, to be sold bad whiskey, and to be exploited in many other ways. Soon the freedom of the Indian would be gone forever.

For several years Sitting Bull, an Indian medicine

man, had been preaching hate and fear of the white man. He had watched Indians driven from their lands. He had seen treaty after treaty broken. He had seen thousands of his people ruined by border ruffians, whiskey smugglers, and disease spreaders. It was time to make a stand! Sitting Bull called together the powerful war chiefs of the great Sioux nation: Crazy Horse, Gall, Black Moon, Spotted Tail, American Horse, Rain-in-the-Face, as well as many other lesser chiefs. Once again the Sioux took to the war path.

By 1876 the government had decided to make a final effort to round up the Sioux tribes and once and for all force them to the reservations. Three different commands were to take part: one to march north into the valley of the Powder River under General Crook (called "Gray Fox" by the Indians); a second under General Gibbon to march to the far western part of the territory; and a third under General Custer (called "Yellow Hair" by the Indians), to march westward from Fort Lincoln. Sitting Bull's forces were to be crushed in this three-pronged attack.

Early in the morning of May 17, 1876, Custer led his full regiment of twelve troops from Fort Lincoln. Custer had with him his bachelor brother, Captain Tom Custer; his brother-in-law, Lieutenant Calhoun; a younger brother, Boston Custer; and a nephew, Autie Reed. These last two relatives were civilians who were with Custer on vacation. All were killed in the battle soon to be fought. Custer's objective was to attack a force of several hundred Indians at a village on the Little Bighorn River, crush all resistance, and force the Indians to surrender. Custer planned to split his regiment into three groups and to attack the village from three sides.

On June 22, at evening camp, Custer gave his final orders. Major Reno took three troops and Indian scouts; Captain Benteen took three troops and the troop in charge of the pack train. Custer kept the remaining five troops under his immediate command, and the commands separated. During the next three days, the three forces approached the village from three different directions, separated by many miles. On the morning of June 26, they were to converge on the village.

Unfortunately, Custer had no way of knowing that Major Reno had already engaged the Indians and had been defeated, losing over half his command. And Custer had no way of knowing that there were not several hundred warriors in the village — there were several thousand, many of them armed with the latest repeating rifles and all mounted on fast ponies. The stage had been set for disaster.

On the morning of June 26, Custer, with his five troops —204 enlisted men, 13 officers, 4 Indian scouts, 1 civilian scout, and 3 civilians—led his men towards the Indian village, assuming that Reno and Benteen were approaching at other points. Although no one can be sure, Custer soon must have realized that neither Reno nor Benteen had been able to reach the village. Indians by the thousands began to pour from the village, and troopers moved towards high ground to make a stand.

Custer quickly sent an order to Captain Benteen to come to his aid. The orderly carrying the message—the last man to see Custer alive—delivered the message, but Benteen did not ride to the relief of Custer. No one knows why. Many have thought it was due to ill-feeling between the two men, but it is hard to believe he could have sacrificed 225 men to his dislike of Custer.

No one knows exactly what took place on the hill overlooking the Little Bighorn River. Reno and Benteen both heard fighting in the distance, but the sound of firing soon became fainter and fainter and then ceased altogether.

There were no known survivors; the only living thing found on the battlefield was a buckskin sorrel called Comanche, the personal mount of one of Custer's captains. Until his death in 1880, this horse was the mascot of the Seventh Cavalry.

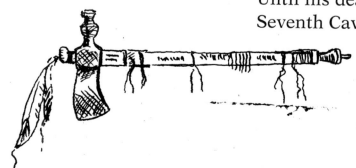

William Frederick Cody
(Buffalo Bill)

1846-1917

JAMES L. VLASATY

X

William Frederick Cody
(Buffalo Bill)

1846–1917

One man who helped to bring the American West to the people of the world was William Frederick Cody, better known as "Buffalo Bill." Cody was an army scout, Indian fighter, showman, and gentleman—as well as a hunter of buffalo, which earned him the name Buffalo Bill. He was born on February 26, 1846, the fourth of eight children, in LeClaire, Iowa. His father, Isaac Cody, a restless, ambitious, energetic man, like most men of the time, aspired to take his family to California to share in the supposed fortunes to be made in the gold fields. They had traveled only as far as Iowa when Buffalo Bill was born.

When Cody was six, one of his older brothers was thrown from a horse and killed. This death so upset the family that the father soon decided to resume the journey west. The family settled in Salt Creek Valley, about 20 miles from Leavenworth, Kansas.

Cody's father became involved in a controversy over slavery and was forced to leave his family. Taking only Will with him, he settled in Lawrence. During the winter of 1854-55, the family was practically destitute, since Isaac had no job and no money to send to them. Will went back home and helped by hunting rabbits and birds. His father died in 1857.

By the age of 11 Will Cody was a good rider and an expert marksman. He had seen and admired cavalrymen from the nearby U.S. Army post, as well as Indian chiefs from the tribes that came to trade at the post.

During this period the Conestoga wagon, which could carry three and a half tons of merchandise, was the basis of the westward freight service. When young Will Cody first saw a train of these wagons being outfitted, he longed to join them. With his mother's consent, he was given his first steady job by a Mr. Majors, one of the partners in the freight company of Russell, Majors, and Waddell. His job was to carry messages from one wagon to another along the weary march. The salary was 40 dollars a month, to be paid to his mother.

Traveling with the wagon train, young Cody paid his first visit to Fort Laramie in Wyoming. Here he became acquainted with the Sioux, Arapaho, and Cheyenne Indians, whose settlements surrounded the adobe walls of the old fort. Here Cody also met the famous scouts Kit Carson and Jim Bridger, and decided that he, too, would someday be a scout.

The company prospered in the freight hauling business and later started the Pony Express to carry mail across the western continent. On April 3, 1860, the first two pony express riders set out, one from St. Joseph, Mis-

souri, westward, the other from Sacramento, California, eastward. This work fascinated Will Cody, and Mr. Russell later gave him a route extending from Red Buttes to Three Crossings in Montana. Cody at this time was only 14, and while serving as a pony express rider, had many thrilling and narrow escapes from both outlaws and Indians. Through the Pony Express, Cody met still another famous frontiersman, Wild Bill Hickok. Cody stayed on as a rider until the telegraph made the Pony Express obsolete less than 16 months after it began.

When Will Cody was 18, his mother died. Since his orphaned sisters needed financial help, he took a job with a wagon train and sent money to them for several years. This characteristic gesture grew into a habit later in life, when his Wild West Show became profitable.

Although Cody considered the Civil War a disgrace to the nation, he enlisted in the 7th Kansas Regiment in 1864. Cody served as a scout and as a dispatch rider, but later was detached for hospital duty for unexplained reasons. It was while serving as an orderly in St. Louis that he met Louisa Frederici. Nearly a year later, on March 6, 1866, they were married.

Although they were very much in love, their personalities and interests were entirely different: she, a prim, properly brought up French girl; Cody, a raw product of the West. To please his wife, Cody for a time gave up the plains and mountains and set himself up in the hotel business at Salt Creek, Kansas. But Cody was both too generous and too lavish a spender to be a businessman. He soon sold the hotel and left for Salina, Kansas, to look for a job. There he again met Wild Bill Hickok, who was working as a scout for the army. Cody applied for a similar position and became a scout under General George A. Custer.

Cody served as an army scout for a short time and then got the job that earned him his nickname. The Union Pacific Railroad had brought hundreds of men out West to lay track, and these men had to be fed. Cody was hired to supply buffalo for meat at a salary of $500.00 a month.

Cody was an experienced hunter. In 17 months he is said to have killed 4,280 buffalo. From then on he was "Buffalo Bill."

The 1870s saw the "Wild West" become a world-wide craze. Almost overnight, it became a land of heroes, a lawless land where men hunted gold and buffalo and fought savages and bandits. From the beginning of the craze, the name "Buffalo Bill" stood above all the rest. With his reputation as a scout and buffalo hunter and with his ornately fringed and beaded buckskins, Buffalo Bill Cody became a living symbol of the "Wild West."

The man who made Buffalo Bill a western hero was Ned Buntline, a dime-novel writer. In a few short years, Buntline filled hundreds of pages with the adventures of Buffalo Bill. It didn't matter that these adventures were mostly fiction or wild exaggerations of real events. The books became best sellers and Buffalo Bill's name became famous all over the world.

Part of the "Wild West" craze was buffalo hunting. While Ned Buntline was spinning out his tales of the legendary Buffalo Bill, the real Buffalo Bill was becoming a guide to the rich, famous, and influential men who wanted to hunt buffalo.

In the fall of 1871, General Phil Sheridan engaged Cody to take a group of his friends on a buffalo hunt. This hunt was so successful that the "dudes" (as they were called) invited Buffalo Bill to visit them later in New York. Then, early in 1872, when Cody was just 26, the Grand Duke Alexis of Russia requested that Buffalo Bill guide him and his party on a buffalo hunt. This hunt, too, was a success, and since it was arranged for a member of one of the ruling families of Europe, it was hailed by the press of the world.

But the novelty of buffalo hunting soon wore off, and Cody again found himself out of work. Happily, it was at this time that Buffalo Bill was to visit New York City as a guest of the men he had guided in 1871. Cody arrived late in 1872 and was entertained by some of the richest and most influential men in the city.

During his six week visit to New York City, he went with Ned Buntline to see a dramatization of one of the dime novelist's stories, *Buffalo Bill*. The play was an instant success and ran for weeks. But Buntline saw a way to improve it. Why use an actor to portray Buffalo Bill when you could use Buffalo Bill himself? Buffalo Bill, having no job and no prospects for a job, agreed to act in person in the plays portraying his life on the plains. This decision was to change Cody from a man of the West to a man of the stage.

After several delays, due to Buntline's poor management, the first stage play starring Buffalo Bill opened on December 18, 1872, in Chicago. The cast included Ned Buntline and an old friend, "Texas Jack" Omohundro. Although it was off to a poor start, Buffalo Bill's popularity made it a financial success. After several weeks in Chicago, the show moved on to St. Louis, Cincinnati, Albany, Boston, and New York City.

The show continued on the road, but in Springfield, Massachusetts, in 1876, Cody received a telegram from his wife saying that his son, Kit Carson Cody (named after the famous scout), was seriously ill. The family was living in Rochester, New York, and Cody rushed home. Sadly, the child, not yet six, died soon thereafter. This was a great personal tragedy to Buffalo Bill, since Kit was an only son. But the show was heavily booked, and, with a heavy heart, Cody resumed his tour.

When the show closed at last, Cody again took up duties for General Wesley Merritt as an army scout. It

was during this time that the most widely publicized adventure in his career as a scout took place—the duel with Chief Yellow Hand.

Trouble was still brewing with the Indians, especially the Sioux, who had never willingly submitted to the treaties of 1868. General Merritt was trying to keep the Cheyennes from joining forces with the Sioux and had set a trap for them. Cody was leading a small group of scouts in advance when the Cheyennes walked into the trap. In the first attack by the soldiers, Buffalo Bill was cut off from his men and found himself facing a young Indian. Both fired. Cody's shot pierced the Indian's leg as well as the pony's heart. But suddenly the scout's horse stepped into a gopher hole throwing Cody to the ground. Buffalo Bill jumped to his feet, grabbed his rifle, and killed the Indian, who was identified later as a young Cheyenne chief, Yellow Hand. News accounts, novels, and other publicity turned this duel into a lasting legend.

Six weeks after the duel, Cody left the army and returned to the East as a hero. There he joined "Arizona John" Burke, who served for years as Buffalo Bill's great press agent.

Cody now had visions of a show that would depict all aspects of life on the plains. The Wild West Show, as Cody imagined it, would be presented as a circus, in large auditoriums, arenas, and the outdoors with cowboys, Indians, and spectacular events depicting western life.

In June 1882 Cody was asked to stage a show in North Platte, Nebraska, for their 4th of July celebration. Cody gathered together cowboy friends, hired a number of Indians, bought the old Deadwood stagecoach, and enacted a stagecoach holdup and other western events. The show was a sensation.

Cody immediately began to make plans to take the show on tour. The first appearance of the "Wild West, Rocky Mountain, and Prairie Exhibition" opened at the Fair Grounds in Omaha on May 17, 1883. From then until 1912, the show grew and was a financial success, with such people as Dr. A. W. Carver, Captain A. H. Bogardus, Gordon W. (Pawnee Bill) Lillie, Major Frank North, Annie Oakley, and later the Indian Medicine Man, Sitting Bull, appearing in person.

Buffalo Bill's Wild West Show, as it was now billed, was under the able management of Nate Salsbury. It was viewed by millions as it visited nearly every city of any size in the United States.

In 1887 the show made a triumphal tour of England, which was then celebrating the Golden Jubilee of Queen Victoria. After opening in London in the spring, it played before large crowds everywhere for nearly a year. The Wild West Company returned to New York in the spring of 1888, opened on Staten Island, and had a season even more successful than its first season in the New York area.

The show then returned to Europe for a continental tour, timed to coincide with the Paris Exposition of 1889. After spending the summer in Paris, the show toured the south of France and then moved on to Italy and Germany.

Returning to the United States, the show once more began to tour American cities. In 1902 Buffalo Bill took the Wild West Show back to Europe for a four-year stay. These later tours were managed by James A. Bailey, of circus fame, as Salsbury was too ill to travel.

By 1912 it was all over. Salsbury and Bailey, the two managers who had made the show a financial success, were dead. Of the millions of dollars the show had made, none remained. Generous as always, Buffalo Bill had spent his share lavishly on friends and family. What little he invested, he invested badly. Nobody, least of all Buffalo Bill, ever knew how much money had passed through his hands.

At 66, tired and sick, the greatest showman of the era was broke. The year before, in 1911, his old friend, "Pawnee Bill," had come to his rescue, combining his show with Buffalo Bill's for a "farewell tour," as it was advertised. The first season, 1911-12, was a success—the crowds thought this was their last opportunity to see

Buffalo Bill. But business began to fall off during their second "farewell," and creditors closed the show.

Cody did not have the ability or the strength to carry on alone. Buffalo Bill acted in one movie (which was never popular), and later signed on to appear with the Sells-Floto Circus. Too ill to ride, he appeared during the performance driving a team of white horses hitched to a phaeton. This hurt Cody's pride, but he was broke and needed money. In 1914 Cody, still in debt, left the circus for the Miller Bros. 101 Ranch Show and forced himself into the saddle once again. Two years later, at the age of 70, he was still appearing in every parade and performance, even though he usually had to be helped on and off his horse.

Buffalo Bill's last appearance was in Portsmouth, Virginia, on November 11, 1916. Too ill to go on, he was ordered home by his doctor. On his way to his sister's home in Denver, he stopped off in Chicago to see if he could raise money among his friends. They could see that he had only a short time to live and kindly advised him to forget his debts and continue on to Denver. He collapsed in Glenwood Springs, Colorado, and was then taken to his sister's home in Denver. Buffalo Bill, the most famous of all the frontiersmen, died on January 10, 1917.